Prophetic Liturgy

Prophetic Liturgy

Toward a Transforming Christian Praxis

TÉRCIO BRETANHA JUNKER

PICKWICK *Publications* · Eugene, Oregon

PROPHETIC LITURGY
Toward a Transforming Christian Praxis

Pickwick Publications
An Imprint of Wipf and Stock Publishers
199 W. 8th Ave., Suite 3
Eugene, OR 97401

www.wipfandstock.com

ISBN 13: 978–1-62032–956-6

Cataloguing-in-Publication Data

Junker, Tércio Bretanha

Prophetic liturgy : toward a transforming Christian praxis / Tércio Bretanha Junker, with a foreword by Dwight W. Vogel

xxiv + 160 p. ; 23 cm. Includes bibliographical references.

ISBN 13: 978–1-62032–956-6

1. Liturgics. 2. Sacraments. 3. Ritual. I. Vogel, Dwight II. Title

BV169 J86 2014

Manufactured in the U.S.A.

To my close and extended family, near and far.
Together, we are an authentic prophetic community of faith.

Contents

Foreword

Say to one another, "Come and hear what the word is that comes forth from the Lord." And they come to you as people come, and they sit before you as my people, and they hear what you have to say but they will not do it; for with their lips they show much love, but their heart is set on their gain. And lo' you are to them like one who sings love songs with a beautiful voice and plays well on an instrument, for they hear what you say, but they will not do it. When this comes—and come it will!—then you will know that a prophet has been among you.

Ezekiel 33:30b–33 NRSV

In this book, Tércio Bretanha Junker examines liturgy as itself prophetic, with the capacity to provide a transformative Christian praxis. Indeed, when understood aright, that prophetic transformative role is part of liturgy's essential nature. Known world-wide for his musical contributions to assemblies of the World Council of Churches, he is also an able liturgical theologian with a perspective arising out of his lived experience in both Brazil and the United States. He makes us aware of liturgy's prophetic role in not only providing a counter-cultural voice aware of socio-economic injustice and speaking God's Word to both the empowered and the disempowered but also in mediating God's desire for goodness, life, and beauty. Liturgy both forms and transforms individuals and communities as it facilitate what Junker calls "a living participation in social, political, and economic life" as agents of transformation.

Using liberation theology as a primary source of reference, his own life experience enables him to explore the interrelationship between liturgy, theology, and ethics as they interact with socio-economic justice. Junker is convinced that liturgical practice grounded in a sacramental theology recognizing that interrelationship will naturally facilitate the community of faith's commitment to the social and economic justice that is part of the well-being of all people as well as the created order.

Ritual acts, Junker observes, construct a human consciousness that provides a space in which to actively participate in a world that is both spiritual and concrete. His own experience in the various "languages" of the liturgical arts (music, movement, speech, and the visual) enables him to reflect on the way in which this liturgical matrix can bring to birth and nourish both individual and communal life including how people live in the world. Thus, Junker insists that prophetic communities of faith taking seriously both the sources and essential character of their liturgical praxis should recognize that liturgy embraces religious-political-cultural-social-economic realities. In this book, he hosts a conversation between biblical-theological foundations, historical-cultural backgrounds, and social-political-economic contexts as foundations for prophetic praxis. Within that context, he points the way to an engaged prophetic consciousness in sacramental liturgical praxis that juxtaposes the values of Christian tradition, the commitment to God's call, and a hunger and thirst to be actively Christian in the world.

Junker insists that the subjective spiritual world must not be disconnected from the concrete living world and that liturgical praxis should facilitate the community's awareness of its biblical and historical foundations with attentiveness to the transformative resonance with which prophetic Christian liturgical practices pursue justice and reconciliation in the world. For Junker, liturgy is a visible and practical "Jubilee," even in the presence of injustice and oppression. He issues a clarion call that, through prophetic liturgy, communities of faith can experience a transformative process that compels them to be agents of radical societal transformation.

The key to this is Junker's seminal concept of "a matrix of total sacramental rituality." In prophetic sacramental liturgy, he discerns a transformative reality within specific given cultures in which God's gifts (as represented in such primary symbols as bread, wine, and water) are given, received, and reciprocated through reincorporation in mission. Junker understands these symbols both to embody and put into effect a transformative sacramental reality. In these cyclical ritual actions, he points us to a sacramental matrix that affirms God's role in working for justice and wholeness in the whole creation while nurturing the spiritual life of the celebrating community, valuing each community's cultural context, and involving communities of faith in the prophetic task of social-political-economic transformation.

In the pages that follow, Junker will insist that every liturgical practice should be "fully ritual, fully sacramental, and fully corporate." This matrix of total sacramental rituality includes the foundational elements of the prophetic dimension of liturgy: theology, culture, and ethics. Junker's contribution to current sacramental and liturgical theology and praxis is his articulation of the trinitarian affinity between God's action and prophetic practice, Jesus' own ministry and Christian vocation, and the work of the Holy Spirit and social-political-economic vision.

Such is the prophetic nature of liturgy. The message of this book is Junker's liberative love song about the inherent capacity of liturgy to be transformative. This dimension of liturgy is frequently ignored or trivialized by churches caught in the economic web woven by the culture around them. Those who are open to hearing the voice of the Holy Spirit in what Tércio Bretanha Junker has written will know that a prophet has been among us.

Dwight W. Vogel, OSL
Pilgrim Place, Claremont, California
Ernest and Bernice Styberg Professor Emeritus of Worship and Preaching,
Garrett-Evangelical Theological Seminary
Evanston, Illinois

Preface

SINCE I ARRIVED IN the United States, coming from Brazil in 1997, I have had the opportunity to participate in many different communities of faith. In those moments of worship, I was able to participate in a variety of worship styles (as they are described in this culture) such as: African American, White, Multicultural, Hispanic, Reconciling Church, and Contemporary Church. I have attended mainly Protestant churches, but I have also had the opportunity to attend services, in Jewish, Roman Catholic, and Orthodox traditions as well. The differences between all of the styles of worshipping are not just made evident by the place, or the language, or the theology; but also, probably even more importantly, by the people who come to experience a sacramental encounter with God, with themselves, and with others. Inevitably, this is a direct connection between the liturgy and the social, economic, educational, and cultural backgrounds of each celebrating community. The liturgy serves as a reflection of the particular character of each community. For each of them one could describe a distinct way of performing the readings from Scripture, singing the hymns and songs (performance and style), addressing words to the community (theology, formal or informal), praying and praising God (extemporaneous or written), proclaiming the Word; wearing liturgical vestments or not and ways in which rites are performed and symbols valued. All of these topics have provided me with helpful elements to form a deep and insightful dialogue about how these communities find and shape the multi-levels of religious languages in their celebrations, and how those languages affect participants as they celebrate together and go out as agents of transformation in the world. I would also add to this list of communities of faith two other significant groups in which I have had the opportunity to celebrate inspirational and transformative liturgical experiences: Christian Theological Seminary (Indianapolis, IN) and Garrett-Evangelical Theological Seminary

(Evanston, IL). The combination of all of these experiences, added to my previous liturgical experiences in Brazil, and in some other Latin American countries, as well as my engagements with the World Council of Churches (WCC) as member of the Assembly Worship Committee in the capacity of Assistant Music Director (9th Assembly, in Porto Alegre, Brazil, 2006) and currently appointed as Music Director for the 10th WCC Assembly for the upcoming assembly in October-November, 2013, have adjusted my liturgical perspective from a local, cloistered, and isolated community to a more global, open, and welcoming celebrating community. In all of these life-religious experiences, I have had the opportunity to see in the flesh both the beauty and the value of human relationships, and the degenerating and scandalous reality of some human *pathos*. Those relationships and experiences all constituted in me insightful references for the development of this book. To all of them I am deeply grateful.

In a real sense, the process of writing this book began long ago, when I was first introduced to the liturgical realm, back in the early 1980s. By that time, Latin American liberation theology was in full bloom and challenging the theological understanding and praxis of both the institutional church and local congregations. In the process of my liturgical theological formation, questions gradually emerged, arousing in me a compelling desire to search for answers that could suit my underdeveloped—yet hungry—theological and liturgical mind. Some of these questions still echo within me, and many others have joined them over the years. This book is a result of my longstanding personal search for reasonable and responsible alternatives.

My theological understanding is inevitably grounded in my own context: the Latin American liberation theology perspective. This undoubtedly limits the approach and analysis of my arguments. Since the conceptual and interdisciplinary assumptions are taken from a particular theological standpoint, the present book is more generally geared toward people who are open to and challenged by this theological approach despite their geographical location.

There is risk in presenting an option for prophetic praxis, in that it may go beyond the comfort zone of a community and engender spiritual and political alienation. The most challenging ethical issue in this book is to provide the worshiping community with prophetic awareness of socio-economic injustice, while at the same time preserving that community's historical-cultural identity, its religious values, and its spirituality. Prophets are often regarded as counter voices, or counter-cultural voices who speak God's Word to the weak, the oppressed, the marginalized, and the helpless. In addition, the prophet seeks to mediate God's desire for goodness, life, and beauty. This is a message that not every Christian in the world wants to hear, let alone be challenged by.

The purpose of this book is to inquire into the prophetic dimension of the liturgy. Within this broad topic, I focus on the contributions of prophetic liturgy towards the transformation of unjust socio-economic systems. Some of the incipient questions that arise include: How can a liturgy be prophetic? What are the biblical, historical, theological, and contemporary components for a prophetic liturgy? How can liturgy form and transform individuals and communities? In which sense does the liturgy facilitate a living participation in social, political, and economic life? What does liturgy have to do with socio-economic justice? How does prophetic liturgy engage the community as agent of transformation? Could the way Christian communities celebrate challenge them to be agents of transformation?

These questions imply the importance and relevance of this book, which is to explore the interrelationship between liturgy and theology as they interact with socio-economic justice. Using liberation theology as foundation, I focus on the particular issues that describe and critique the liturgical praxis of the church regarding its socio-economic understanding of itself. A constructive dialogue between Christian liturgy and theology will provide the basic framework for an in-depth analysis of the present time. The argument will be centered on the conception that liturgical praxis and theological grounding should naturally facilitate a socio-economic consciousness in the whole community of faith. Because of the importance of social science as a tool for social analysis, I also include a discussion on how social science can be a means of mediation for a transforming and engaging Christian community that is committed to the social and economic justice and well-being of all people, and the created order.

Acknowledgments

THIS BOOK COULD NOT have been completed without the support and solidarity of numerous individuals, church communities, and institutions. It is not possible to express satisfactorily in words my deepest gratitude to the three committee members of the doctoral defense at Garrett-Evangelical Theological Seminary who, in one way or in another, provided me with the necessary academic support and encouragement: Dr. Dwight W. Vogel, Dr. Ruth C. Duck, and Dr. Ernest Byron Anderson. They are part of my educational trajectory not only in the cognitive sense, but also as human beings who have taught me to live a sacramental life committed to God and to the well-being of humanity. I am profoundly grateful to Dr. Vogel, who with patience, enthusiasm, and skillful scholarship in theology, liturgy, and music—which coupled with an abiding concern for justice and for peace in the world—encouraged my research endeavors. The generous spirit and open heart of both Dr. Vogel, and his wife Dr. Linda J. Vogel, will be remembered as a gift, which in return, I offer my commitment to scholarship and sacramental life.

This book is the result of a revisiting process to my doctoral dissertation on Liturgical Studies. In that process, Dr. Rufus Burrow Jr., Indiana Professor of Christian Thought and Professor of Theological Social Ethics at Christian Theological Seminary, Indianapolis, Indiana, deserves a special word of gratitude. His patience and vigorous dedication reading the complete manuscript, with perceptive and insightful feedbacks on the revision process, exceeded my highest expectations. Dr. Burrow is a source of inspiration: he is both a sensitive human being and a mentor who knows what it is to stand up for justice and reject the *evil* forces *wherever they exist*, to use Martin Luther King Jr.'s expression. With him, I express my profound gratitude to the entire community of Christian Theological Seminary, trustees, administration, faculty, and students for their support, encouragement, and inspiration. It has been a great pleasure to work with such a diverse and committed community that does not measure efforts in promoting integrity in scholarship.

Finally, none of this work would have been possible without the love and support of my wife Dr. Débora Junker, our children—seeds of love— Yohana, Louise, and Tércio, and our extended children Helton and Rafael— our sons-in-law (husbands of Yohana and Louise, respectively). To them, my deepest gratitude! To my dear mother and father (both *in memoriam*), my supportive sisters and brothers, and my extended family from my wife's side, who all together, constitute the nest and source of inspiration for my spiritual and academic journeys.

I offer a very deep and special appreciation to my wife, Débora, a brilliant woman, voracious researcher and dedicated professor, mother and an example of determination to me and our children, with whom I share my secrets, my dreams, my achievements and frustrations, my spirituality, my unconditional love, and with whom I have shared, during our thirty one years of marriage, a biblical passage that has accompanied us since the very beginning of our life together: "Each one helps the other, saying to one another, 'Take courage!'" (Isa 41:6)

Introduction

LITURGICAL CELEBRATION IS A fruitful ground for teaching/learning processes. Christian liturgical celebrations are places, as ritual acts, for constructing an effective human consciousness in terms of persons being allowed the space to actively participate in the spiritual and concrete world. The variety of languages present in the liturgical experience, such as music, gesture, icons, and words, can facilitate (construct) growth in the Christian life as well as influence the way people live in the world. It follows that the prophetic community of faith must take very seriously the sources and character of its liturgical celebrations, recognizing that the liturgy embraces religious-political-cultural-social-economic realities. Thus, biblical-theological foundations, historical-cultural backgrounds, and social-political-economic contexts are the ultimate foundations for prophetic praxis.[1] Given these premises, an engaged prophetic consciousness in the field of liturgy should function as a built-in response to questions that juxtapose the values of the common Christian tradition, the commitment to God's call, and the hunger and thirst to be actively Christian in the world.

When we approach liturgical praxis with the aforementioned assumption as a theoretical point of reference, we join together in an engaging learning process in which both historical-liturgical foundations and sound theological principles will need to be emphasized. The celebration will necessarily be structured into a dynamic correlation of the "common Christian tradition," the here and now, and the eschatological dimensions of the liturgy. By "common Christian tradition," I mean that which has been, and continues to be, essential to Christian liturgical praxis and thoughts throughout the Christian historical trajectory. The expression "common Christian tradition" is used here not only in relation to what is common

---

1. See chapter 1 for an explanation on the preference of "praxis" over "practice."

in a denominational sense, but also in relation to what exists in the most remote Christian liturgical praxis. Christian historical identity is related to the imperishable reality of the liturgical Christian tradition. This vision provides the new and transitory without renouncing the historically permanent. This posture is motivated by a strong desire to preserve what was and still is significant to historical Christian identity. As such, the liturgical celebration represents the central place where identity is embodied. There are many expressive liturgical symbols, gestures, acts, words, and texts that must be saved from passing into anonymity. How can people appreciate the tremendous symbolic value of liturgical treasures that have survived for years and years? How can these symbolic treasures be preserved for future generations if we fail to keep them alive in our regular celebrations? In order to address these questions, we must look in as many different directions as possible.

Furthermore, in order to insure commitment to God's call and facilitate prophetic response to the cries and sufferings of the world, the liturgy needs to assess its direct connections to biblical foundations and to the cultural traditions of the worshiping community. Prophetic liturgical praxis requires the acknowledgement that the subjective spiritual world is not disconnected from the concrete living world. In other words, the whole process of celebrating liturgy should facilitate the community's awareness of its biblical foundations, the Christian historical trajectory, a consciousness of its cultural unity, and attentiveness to the transformative resonance of prophetic Christian liturgical praxis seeking socio-economic justice in the world.

Thus, a prophetic Christian community should pursue eagerly the need to read reality, evaluate its effects, and then act intentionally. The key elements that sustain the Christian community towards this goal are: Scripture, sacraments, and ethics. Scripture is the reference point for reading the present reality; the sacraments are the liminal places where the community evaluates itself and the world, and finds strength for its existence; and ethics focuses on the social, political, economic, and cultural engagement of the prophetic church. The vocation of a prophetic community is to be active in the pursuit of justice and reconciliation. This engagement reflects what could be understood as a possible means toward the visible and practical Jubilee in the midst of the unjust, undesirable, and oppressive socio-economic systems in which we live. My argument is that, through a prophetic liturgy, the community of faith experiences a transformative process and is thereby compelled to be an agent of radical transformation in society. Of course, immediately the question arises: How can this be achieved? My answer is that it can be achieved through a *matrix of total sacramental rituality*. A brief comment will explain what I mean.

My assertion about the *matrix* is that, as the community celebrates a prophetic liturgy, it experiences a transformative reality in which God's gifts are separated, received, and reciprocated in cyclical ritual actions that, first, affirm God's project of justice and life for the whole creation; second, support the community's spiritual life; third, value the community's cultural context; and fourth, challenge the community to be a prophetic agent of transformation.

This is a complex liturgical assumption that incorporates in itself concepts of biblical, theological, anthropological, cultural, economic, political, religious, and ethical realities. The aim is always engagement in prophetic praxis. As a result, the prophetic community of faith experiences the juxtaposition of three levels of ritual communication: spiritual/transcendent-language (theology); socio/cultural-language (culture); and political/economic-language (ethics). The prophetic community is thereby called to act with commitment against many different factors that compromise the dignity of human beings and the stability of the created order. It is by celebrating total sacramental rituality that symbolic exchange will have the most fundamental expression of justice and transformation. The prophetic community is a transformative community—transforming, and always being transformed, as a visible sign of symbolic exchange.

In short, this book explores the liturgy as prophetic mediation for transforming and engaging the Christian community in seeking socio-economic justice for all people, everywhere. In part, this will require a critical analysis of biblical, theological, historical, and contemporary perspectives in relevant liturgical sources, with attention to the need to achieve socio-economic justice. This will uncover foundational elements to construct and conceptualize the potentiality that a prophetic liturgy has for transformative praxis in church and society.

The argument of this book assumes that liturgical texts are embodied discourses. The "speech-act" theory confirms this statement. The text is an embodied "speech-act," which carries with it the intention of an author. The text as a communicative action embodies an intent directed towards a receiver. John L. Austin's language act theory, echoed in many hermeneutics theorists, states that texts have an embodied locution (propositional content), an illocutionary force (a context of action in which the text does something), and a perlocutionary effect (an impact upon the receiver). Kevin J. Vanhoozer summarizes Austin's language act theory as follows: "(1) the locutionary act: uttering words (e.g., saying the word 'Hello'); (2) the illocutionary act: what we do in saying something (e.g., greeting, promising, commanding, etc.); (3) the perlocutionary act: what we bring about by saying something (e.g., persuading, surprising)."[2]

Fundamentally, this book brings theological, socio-economic, political, and anthropological issues into dialogue with liturgical sacramental studies in the hope of making it possible to understand more clearly the essence and necessity of prophetic action. The aim of such action is to proclaim and work toward the Kingdom of God. Moreover, since prophetic criticism is grounded in ideological critiques, it certainly can be correlated with historical, political, and ideological criticism. This is an inevitable assumption, as prophetic actions address particular conditions of human existence.

In the pages that follow, we will see the necessity of discovering multiple languages in which the complex system of Christian identity has its roots. The latter includes its theological formulation, its liturgical expression, its political-ideological function, and its ethical relevance. Prophetic liturgy as transforming/engaging Christian praxis requires the understanding that living liturgical celebration is a communal act in which one both receives and gives.

Chapter 1 examines the biblical and historical foundations for prophetic praxis. From the biblical perspective there will be emphasis on the prophetic praxis as witnessed by the Old Testament, and coupled with Jesus' New Testament commitment to human well-being through his announcement of God's kingdom of peace, love, justice and equality. From the historical perspective, the focus will be on the ethical messages delivered by those who heard the cry of the needy, the poor, and the ones who suffered unjust socio-economic systems from time to time and gave a prophetic response. With the contemporary perspective in mind, the focus turns to conversations with current approaches that take seriously the socio-economic order and the imperative of global transformation. In the process, there is affirmation that Christian prophetic liturgical praxis has its concreteness in the community's social-political-economic consciousness.

---

2. Vanhoozer, *Is There a Meaning in This Text?*, 209. See also Chauvet, *Symbol and Sacrament*, 130–33.

Chapters 2 and 3 are the pivotal chapters of the book. They provide the core understanding of the prophetic dimension of the liturgy as means towards the transformation of church and world, as well as the mediation of economic-social justice. The focus of chapter 2 is on the sacraments as means of transformation. The chapter explores the idea that sacramental praxis provides a pattern for our day to day living. From the perspective of living a faithful Christian sacramental life in the world, the community of faith commits itself to a liturgical spirituality, which infuses life into the liturgy in such a way that everyday life becomes sacramental. This chapter also makes the case that the sacraments provide the ideal means for a person to experience the grace of God for the sake of God's mission in the world. In addition, the sacraments have significance beyond the ceremony of the ritual itself. I argue that it is through the sacramental life of the church that Christ greets us, reveals his paschal mystery, assures God's promised blessings, and affirms the eschatological presence of the Holy Spirit revealing God's kingdom. With this in mind it can be said that by participating in the sacraments, especially baptism and the Eucharist, the community of faith is nourished, strengthened, and united with Christ's body, and prepared to do mission. For me, sacrament is a powerful, transformative mediation that consists of more than mere signs of bread, wine, and water. We will see that these are more than symbols; they actually embody and put into effect the promises they claim to render.

Chapter 3 will focus on the mission work of the people. It explores the community's vocation as an agent of transformation, pointing to the Trinitarian community as the foundation of this action. This chapter also challenges the community of faith to be in dialogue with the social sciences. I make the case that the fields of liturgy and the social sciences need to be in dialogue with each other, searching together for responsible ways to connect common key elements, which promote militant Christian praxis in the world. The aim is to explore how Christian communities might engage with key social science methods in ways that could make them absorb and connect the complex languages of these sciences to their faith and to their real lives. The issue at stake in chapter three is how worshiping communities can better understand their socio-economic system in order to recognize the signs of good and evil, life and death in them. Such recognition better positions these communities to act critically and prophetically, seeking the transformation of the socio-economic system and proclaiming justice for all.

Chapter 4 brings us to what I call total sacramental rituality, and presents the theoretical framework for it. Included here is a discussion regarding the level of symbolic exchange as it might be perceived in a postmodern perspective, in the prophetic dimension of the sacrament, and in levels of ritual language utilized by theology, culture, and ethics. The chapter makes the case that the principle of suspicion becomes a new paradigm for all kinds of understandings, including the understanding of theological, philosophical, sociological, political, and economic phenomena that pertains to human postmodern existentiality. Here I argue that liturgical praxis are not exempt from postmodern incursions. The discussion turns next to exploring possible answers to the question: How can we live the sacramentality of Christian existence prophetically in a world that seems to be far from spiritual and communal consciousness? Core concepts such as symbols, cultural sensitivity, common Christian tradition, identity, and memory are introduced into the discussion. Chapter 4 also examines theoretical references for the matrix of total sacramental rituality, in which the community of faith experiences the juxtaposition of three levels of ritual communication: spiritual/transcendent-language (theology); cultural/contextual-language (culture); and socio/political/economic-language (ethics).

Chapter 5 introduces the sacramental paradigm (*matrix*) connecting the key themes for the prophetic dimension of the liturgy. Based on the tripartite schema presented in chapter four, this concluding chapter develops a paradigm for the prophetic praxis of the church. As noted above, this is what I call the matrix of total sacramental rituality. My primary assumption is that every single liturgical experience ought to be fully ritual, fully sacramental, and fully corporate. Rituality brings sacredness; sacramentality brings a sense of belonging; and corporate participation brings the desire for sharing. This matrix of total sacramental rituality is inclusive of the three foundational elements of the prophetic dimension of liturgy: theology, culture, and ethics. This is a complex liturgical assumption that incorporates in itself concepts of theological, anthropological, cultural, economic, political, religious, and ethical realities as it engages in prophetic praxis. Given this frame of reference, this book is primarily concerned with the affinity between: God's action and prophetic praxis; Jesus' ministry and Christian vocation; and The Holy Spirit and social-political-economic vision.

1

Foundational Concepts
for Prophetic Praxis

> For thus says the Lord to the house of Israel: Seek me and live;
> Seek good, and not evil, that you may live; . . . Hate evil and love
> good, and establish justice in the gate; . . . Let justice roll down like
> waters, and righteousness like an ever-flowing stream. (Amos 5:4,
> 14, 15, 24)[1]

A CHRISTIAN COMMUNITY CHARACTERIZED by historical sensitivity and
sustained by a coherent biblical-theological understanding has the potential for transforming itself and the world. Celebrating or worshiping communities, in which human relationships are manifested, are fertile grounds
for the emergence and development of transformative patterns. This provides the foundation for a prophetic Christian community. The context for
the life of such a community is its past, its present, and its envisioning of a
better future, one where the sufferings and the accomplishments of its own
people, as well as those beyond it, are cared for and celebrated.

A prophetic Christian community can be built in response to the need
for an open space where transformation and justice can happen. From the
prophetic perspective, we do liturgical theology when we acknowledge
that in liturgy, especially in sacramental celebration, the human *pathos* and

---

1. Unless otherwise noted, all scriptural passages are from the New Revised Standard
Version of the Bible.

God's *ethos*[2] encounter each other in a demanding claim for transformation with justice. Indeed, there is an urgent need for the prophetic celebrating community to be an agency of proclamation and a prophetic voice that cries out for liberation from all kinds of situations in which the inalienable right to human dignity and their potential for development is undermined. The vocation and contribution of the celebrating community is to affirm the right of every individual, regardless of class, citizenship, race, gender, sexual orientation or age, to live in dignity and to explore the limits of human possibilities. The aim is for everyone to be able to participate in establishing a new social order where freedom, justice, peace, and the experience of full humanity prevail in the world.

In the diverse, global, individualist, competitive and selfish context of this era, the Christian community, with this understanding of its prophetic vocation, is called to act in ways that reach beyond the limits of common historical and modern Christian stereotypes. A prophetic community should be eager to exert its capacity to interpret reality, to evaluate its effects, and to act consciously. The ability to do this is rooted in a prophetic criticism and a visionary imagination, which contains the strength to transform the undesired order.

In light of the foregoing discussion on prophetic understanding, this chapter will examine the biblical and early Christian foundations for the requirement to establish socio-economic justice through prophetic praxis. It also examines significant prophetic contemporary voices, in particular: Dom Hélder Câmara, Mother Theresa, Martin Luther King, Jr., and Archbishop Oscar Romero. This discussion will be restricted to contributions from four primary sources: the Hebrew prophets; Jesus' prophetic praxis; select early Christian apologists; and the contemporary prophetic praxis. Before proceeding, however, it will be helpful to explore the rationale for use of the term *praxis*.

---

2. I am drawing here on Saliers who gives a helpful explanation on "human pathos" and "divine ethos." He says: "[B]y *pathos* I mean the human suffering of the world. Human emotions and passions . . . By the divine *ethos*, I mean the characteristic manner in which liturgy is self-giving of God to us, the encounter whereby grace and glory find human form. Christian liturgy transforms and empowers when the vulnerability of human pathos is met by the ethos of God's vulnerability in word and sacrament" (Saliers, *Worship as Theology*, 22). For another approach to "divine pathos" and "divine ethos," see Heschel, *The Prophets*, 217–19. Moltmann also quotes Heschel who, according to Moltmann, "called the theology of the Old Testament prophets a 'theology of the divine pathos.'" Moltmann presents God's suffering as a manifestation of love, mercy, and pity. See Moltmann, *The Trinity and the Kingdom*, 25.

The term *praxis* is preferred over *practice* because of the prophetic underpinnings of the word, although in some contexts they may be used interchangeably. Praxis can include the idea of transformative action. In this regard, Paulo Gadotti writes that "transforming *praxis* is essentially creative, daring, critical, and reflexive."[3] Similarly, in *Pedagogy of the Oppressed*, Paulo Freire suggests that the term *praxis* implies critical reflection and transforming action. One of Freire's arguments is that "people will be truly critical if they live the plenitude of the praxis, that is, if their action encompasses a critical reflection which increasingly organizes their thinking and thus leads them to move from a purely naïve knowledge of reality to a higher level."[4] This "higher level"—to perceive the cause of reality—which Freire is talking about, ultimately corresponds to a desire, which is undeniably prophetic: the desire for religious commitment, political engagement and socio-economic transformation on the way to establishing justice—a primary concern of the Hebrew prophets. It is precisely in this sense that praxis means critical reflection and transformative action: hope and action together. In order to present a clear and challenging understanding of prophetic Christian praxis in the present world, the concept of praxis requires the type of passionate and precise definition such as that offered by Gadotti and Freire. Therefore, in my usage, the term *praxis* is always understood as being clearly connected to the prophetic commitment to human well-being by seeking truth, justice, equality, peace, and life for all, not just for some.

It is in this context of critical reflection and transformative action that I will now discuss the biblical, historical, and current ideas which affirm that Christian prophetic liturgical praxis has its grounding in the community's religious-social-political-economic consciousness, leading to existential and social freedom.[5] It is in this context that the community of faith prophesies.

3. Gadotti, *Pedagogy of Praxis*, xvii.

4. Freire, *Pedagogy of the Oppressed*, 112. For more insights on Freirian concept of praxis, see Gadotti, *Pedagogy of Praxis*, ix–xvii.

5. West suggests that existential freedom and social freedom are the two inseparable notions of freedom for prophetic Christianity. They are two necessary conditions "which themselves are both results of past human practice and preconditions for it in the present." In attempting to define the two concepts he says: "Existential freedom is an effect of the divine gift of grace which promises to sustain persons through and finally deliver them from the bondage to death, disease, and despair. Social freedom is the aim of Christian political practice, a praxis that flows from the divine gift of grace; social freedom results from the promotion and actualization of the norms of individuality and democracy. Existential freedom empowers people to fight for social freedom, to realize

CONTRIBUTIONS OF THE HEBREW PROPHETIC TRADITION

It is important to acknowledge that much of the discussion in this and succeeding sections of the book is informed by Rabbi Abraham J. Heschel's work on the Hebrew prophets. In his great book, *The Prophets*, Heschel gives a compelling description of Hebrew prophecy.

> Prophecy is not simply the application of timeless standards to particular human situations, but rather an interpretation of a particular moment in history, a divine understanding of a human situation. Prophecy, then, may be described as exegesis of existence from a divine perspective. Understanding prophecy is an understanding of an understanding rather than an understanding of knowledge; it is exegesis of exegesis . . . Proper exegesis is an effort to understand the philosopher in terms and categories of philosophy, the poet in terms and categories of poetry, and the prophet in terms and categories of prophecy. Prophecy is a way of thinking as well as a way of living.[6]

Prophecy is not about human beings' perspective or understanding of the world. Rather, it is about God's understanding and perspective on what is occurring in the world. It is about the prophet's understanding of the divine perspective. The prophet, on this view, endeavors to convey to the people and the powers God's understanding of what is happening in the world. The prophet conveys God's perspective from the context of her or his own socio-cultural context. This is what Heschel means by the important phrase, "exegesis of existence from a divine perspective." We need a prophetic lens to read and understand the world if we are to be a prophetic community. A correct understanding of the terms and categories of prophetic praxis will foster the community's transformative vocation towards freedom, equality, justice, and peace. Therefore, it is also necessary to establish conceptual parameters for using terms such as "prophet" and "vocation."

According to Heschel, the Hebrew prophets of the eighth century BCE are among the most peculiar and disturbing personalities to ever appear on the stage of history; "the men whose inspiration brought the Bible into

---

its political dimension. Existential freedom anticipates history and is ultimately trans-historical, whereas social freedom is thoroughly a matter of this-worldly human liberation" (see West, *Prophesy Deliverance!*, 18).

6. Heschel, *The Prophets*, xiii–xiv.

being—the men whose image is our refuge in distress, and whose voice and vision sustain our faith."[7] In a broad sense, a prophet is a person who looks at reality with the divine perspective and conveys that perspective to the people. "The prophet regards himself as one who walks together with God," says Heschel.[8] Thus, a prophet is one who *speaks for someone else*. This is what the Hebrew word *navi* (in the plural, *n'vi-im*) means, and this is why the most common expression used by prophets to deliver God's message is, "Thus says the Lord."[9]

Heschel further clarifies the meaning of prophet when he says, "The prophet is a watchman (Hos 9:8), a servant (Amos 3:7; Jer 25:4; 26:5), a messenger of God (Hag 1:13), 'an assayer and tester' of the people's ways (Jer 6:27, RSV); 'whenever you hear a word from my mouth, you shall give them warning from Me' (Ezek 3:17)."[10] Accordingly, through the prophet's words, as Heschel affirms, "the invisible God becomes audible."[11] In like manner, through the prophet's eyes, the invisible God becomes visible. Heschel continues, "Yet his ear is inclined to God. He is a person struck by the glory and presence of God, overpowered by the hand of God. Yet his true greatness is his ability to hold God and man in a single thought."[12] Thus, a prophet is a person with a mission and with the power of word that is not his or her own, but rather the result of a special human sensitivity that allows the individual to be God's mediator and voice to the community. The prophet's eye is focused on to the contemporary scene, while the prophet's ears are inclined to God.[13] As Heschel attests, "the prophet was an individual who said no to his society, condemning its habits and assumptions, its complacency, waywardness, and syncretism. He was often compelled to proclaim the very opposite of what his heart expected. His fundamental objective was to reconcile man and God. Why do the two need reconciliation? Perhaps it is due to man's false sense of sovereignty, to his abuse of freedom, to his aggressive, sprawling pride, resenting God's involvement in history."[14]

---

7. Ibid., ix.

8. Ibid., 38.

9. McKenna, *Prophets*, 16.

10. Heschel, *The Prophets*, 20–21.

11. Ibid., 22.

12. Ibid., 21.

13. Ibid.

14. Ibid., xv.

An example will help to illuminate the point. When we see the economy growing, with enormous wealth and the prosperity in the world, the temptation is to say *yes* to the economic system. But prophets have a different perspective on the way they see reality because they see through divine lens. Therefore, they call upon the people to abandon the *status quo* imposed by those who profit from it most. A prophet would have the ability to perceive and to name the specific problems within the bigger picture of an economic system from which a few people benefit at the expense of the masses.

Prophets have no patience when it comes to the scandalous condition of depriving people of the basic necessities of life. Their ears are inclined to God, and to hearing what God compels them to do to address and to transform the scandalous condition. The prophet Isaiah reminds us of what will happen to those who oppress the people: "Ah, you who make iniquitous decrees, who write oppressive statutes, to turn aside the needy from justice and to rob the poor of my people of their right, that widows may be your spoil, and that you may make the orphans your prey! What will you do on the day of punishment, in the calamity that will come from far away? To whom will you flee for help, and where will you leave your wealth, so as not to crouch among the prisoners or fall among the slain? For all this his anger has not turned away; his hand is stretched out still." (Isa 10:1–4) Commenting on this passage, Gustavo Gutiérrez says, "The prophets condemn every kind of abuse, every form of keeping the poor in poverty or of creating new poor."[15]

Like the strange beings in Ezekiel's vision (Ezek. 1:18), prophets are also said to be *full of eyes*. Picking up on this image of "full of eyes," Humbert of Romans[16] gives a remarkable description of these religious ones,

15. In addition to this passage, Gutiérrez brings a helpful summary list of biblical texts which show the biblical inconformity with the exploitation of those in need. He summarizes: "Fraudulent commerce and exploitation are condemned (Hos 12:8; Amos 8:5; Mic 6:10–11; Isa 3:14; Jer 5:27; 6:12), as well as the hoarding of lands (Mic 3:1–3; Ezek 22:29; Hab 2:5–6), dishonest courts (Amos 5:7; Jer 22:13–17; Mic 3:9–11; Isa 5:23, 10:1–2), the violence of the ruling classes (2 Kgs 23:30, 35; Amos 4:1; Mic 3:1–2; 6:12; Jer 22:13–17), slavery (Neh 5:1–5; Amos 2:6; 8:6), unjust taxes (Amos 4:1; 5:11–12), and unjust functionaries (Amos 5:7; Jer 5:28). In the New Testament oppression by the rich is also condemned, especially in Luke (6:24–25; 12:13–21; 16:19–31; 18:18–26) and in the Letter of James (2:5–9; 4:13–17; 5:16)" (see Gutiérrez, *A Theology of Liberation*, 167).

16. Born around 1200 at Romans, near Valence in France, Humbert of Romans entered the Dominican Order at the end of 1224. According to Tugwell, Humbert of Romans's treatise *On the Formation of Preachers*, "is the most authoritative document from

which I am calling prophets. Here is what he says: "They should have eyes to the rear, to see whether they are being enticed back to the things they have abandoned, and eyes in front, to see whether they are, like the apostles, surpassing themselves in what lies ahead of them, namely spiritual things, and eyes to the left, to see that they do not lose heart when things are difficult, and eyes to the right, to see that they do not become proud when things are going well."[17] Prophets are those whose eyes are focused on what is happening in the context of her or his contemporary scene, and yet the prophet's ears are always open to God.

According to Martin Buber, "every prophet speaks in the actuality of a definite situation."[18] That is to say, the prophet speaks from and to his or her own situation. Thus, in order to understand the words and claims of prophets, we must be acquainted with the situation or context in which they are proclaimed. When the prophet sees the community's *sitz im leben* and, at the same time hears God's word, the prophet becomes caught in an inner struggle. Such one is compelled to cry out for justice and peace, so that when he or she speaks, God is revealed and transforming action is called for.

The Old Testament reveals that the most intense manifestations of prophecy happened in the political context of a monarchy. Interestingly enough, the decline of prophetic activity corresponded with the collapse of that same monarchy. In the Old Testament historical context, one can see that prophetic praxis was marked by conflict with kings. For example: Jeremiah in conflict with Jehoiakim, King of Israel; Nathan confronting David with his sin; Amos being asked to leave the Northern Kingdom because he dared to speak against the king; both Micah and Isaiah severely attacked the political intrigue and religious syncretism of Ahaz; and even in the New Testament, where John the Baptist is seen challenging Herod, and then faces serious consequences. All of these contexts reveal that prophetic voices were addressed primarily to political and religious leaders in response to their failure to properly worship God and to act responsibly toward people's need.[19] As Heschel says, "The prophet is not only a prophet . . . He is also

---

the period on the spirituality and attitudes that are appropriate to these whose vocation it is to be preachers." See Tugwell, *Early Dominicans*, xiii. For a particular interest on Dominican's spirituality, see Tugwell, *Ways of Imperfection*.

17. Quoted from *On the Formation of Preachers* by Simon Tugwell. See Tugwell, *Early Dominicans*, 4–5.

18. Buber, *The Prophetic Faith*, 96.

19. An example from our time comes from the prophetic praxis of Dom Hélder

poet, preacher, patriot, statesman, social critic, moralist."[20] Prophets' voices, then, speak for God in the context of each prophet's own socio-political context. Heschel agrees saying, "The prophet's task is to convey a divine view, yet as a person he *is* a point of view. He speaks from the perspective of God as perceived from the perspective of his own situation."[21] The prophet sees and hears what others do not. What seems minor and acceptable to most people is viewed by the prophet as a state of emergency, and she is outraged by it. Heschel makes the point in a poignant way, saying:

> To us the moral state of society, for all its stains and spots, seems fair and trim; to the prophet it is dreadful. So many deeds of charity are done, so much decency radiates day and night; yet to the prophet satiety of the conscience is prudery and flight from responsibility. Our standards are modest; our sense of injustice tolerable, timid; our moral indignation impermanent; yet human violence is interminable, unbearable, permanent. To us life is often serene, in the prophet's eye the world reels in confusion. The prophet makes no concession to man's capacity. Exhibiting little understanding for human weakness, he seems unable to extenuate the culpability of man . . . The words of the prophet are stern, sour, stinging. But behind his austerity is love and compassion for mankind . . . The prophet is sent not only to upbraid, but also to "strengthen the weak hands and make firm the feeble knees" (Isa 35:3). Almost every prophet brings consolation, promise, and the hope of reconciliation along with censure and castigation. He begins with a message of doom; he concludes with a message of hope.[22]

Prophets, therefore, stand as "counter-voices" to any voice that allows fascination with power, ambition, and self-righteousness which is in opposition to what God requires from us: to do justice, love kindness, and walk humbly with God (Mic 6:8).

Câmara (1909–1999), a Brazilian Roman Catholic Archbishop of Olinda and Recife for whom, according to Julio de Santa Ana, "prophetic mission was more important to him (Dom Hélder) than the priesthood. This option did not make his life any easier. He had to deal with the established authorities, as well as with incomprehension in the ranks of the church, and even among his fellow bishops. All this testifies to his prophetic quality." See Santa Ana, "Priest and Prophet," in *The Promise of Hope: A Tribute to Dom Hélder*, ed. Schipani and Wessels, 12.

20. Heschel, *The Prophets: An Introduction*, x.

21. Ibid., xii.

22. Ibid., 9.

Walter L. Owensby contends that, "the Protestant doctrine of the priesthood of all believers is the prophethood of all believers. To be a part of the believing community is to be among the forthtellers, those who share their concerns about the way the world is and ought to be as God gives them insight."[23] As communities of faith, we are called to be prophetic voices of our time. A prophetic voice is, by definition, "counter-cultural," in the sense that it challenges the way things are, and posits alternatives for human relationships that are radically different from those of dominion of power, exploitation, and oppression. In our prophethood, we are called to challenge society to abandon the culture of sin, oppression, injustice, and war, and to turn faithfully to God's expectations and promises.

From my perspective, the prophetic vocation of the church pushes it to see, to assay, and to denounce concrete systems of evil that promote massive systemic hunger, poverty, economic dependence, pollution, violence, war, injustice and the many other factors that demean the dignity of human beings. The possibility of this prophetic concept being communicated to one of the many different dimensions of Christian praxis is directly related to the visionary element of prophecy. I use the word *visionary* because prophets are sensitized and stimulated by factors that allow them: (1) to hear the past, sincerely reclaiming its memory; (2) to analyze the present, critically proclaiming its redemption; and (3) to envision the future, intensely anticipating its transformation.

The first factor, *to hear the past, sincerely reclaiming its memory*, is a religious enterprise. Memory is the pillar of religious praxis, especially in liturgical Christian contexts. No prophet is able to reclaim memory without considering its religious basis. Paul Connerton presents an interesting approach toward understanding how memory functions in a living society. In his book, *How Societies Remember*, Connerton explores the concept of social memory as a central topic. Concerning this theme, in which past and present are connected, Connerton affirms that, "we may note that images of the past commonly legitimate a present social order."[24] For him, the memory of groups is conveyed and sustained through recollection, performances, bodily praxis, social habits, myths, commemorative ceremonies, the creation of works of art, ritual, legal, and theological texts. A prophetic perspective reclaims memory through God's Word and liturgical actions. The last item will be related to the way Scripture shows prophets reclaiming

---

23. Owensby, *Economics for Prophets*, x.
24. Connerton, *How Societies Remember*, 3.

memory. I will make the case that a prophetic perspective reclaims memory through God's Word and liturgy.

The second factor, *to analyze the present critically, proclaiming its redemption*, is a social enterprise. Prophets are in direct connection with divine entities. As mentioned before, Heschel elucidates this point clearly, when he says that from the perspective of his own social context, the prophet endeavors to relay God's message to the people. The prophet's religiosity is grounded in his or her own situation. This means that prophets are actually multidimensional analysts. They have an intimate relationship with God, and yet their human senses are consciously focused on their social, political, economic, cultural, and religious context. Prophets cannot separate religious realities from human social life. Their life and point of view are a true sacrament in the sense that their words and deeds are true mediations of God's redemptive grace and invisible presence among God's people.

The third factor, *to envision the future, intensely anticipating its transformation*, is a political enterprise. It is here that the issue of our active political-spiritual participation in the life of the world is confronted. It represents our work for justice, mercy, and love while envisioning political transformation for the sake of future generations. Amos' prophetic voice must ring out incessantly in our ears, "I despise your festivals, and I take no delight in your solemn assemblies . . . Take away from me the noise of your songs; I will not listen to the melody of your harps. But let justice roll down like waters, and righteousness like an everflowing stream." (Amos 5:21–24) Patricia Wilson-Kastner helpfully comments that "such a moral life encompasses our relationship with God, our life, and our social relationships."[25] These relationships call for justice and righteousness. Although closely related concepts—indeed we may go so far to say they are two sides of a single coin—we may differentiate justice and righteousness. Justice requires that one be given her or his due. When righteousness is added, it means that one is to be given more than his or her due. Such one is to be given their due in the most respectful, righteous way. Mere justice can be harsh and can be conferred in ways that undermine the dignity of persons. Righteousness requires that justice be dispensed in ways that show compassion and respect for persons. Heschel provides an enlightening commentary on the matter. "Righteousness goes beyond justice. Justice is strict and exact, giving each person his due. Righteousness implies benevolence, kindness,

25. Duck and Wilson-Kastner, *Praising God*, 130. See also Saliers, *Worship as Theology*, 17–90.

and generosity. Justice is form, a state of equilibrium; righteousness has a substantive associated meaning. Justice may be legal; righteousness is associated with a burning compassion for the oppressed."[26] Prophetic praxis has inherent ethical implications. Indeed, the type of prophecy discussed in this book *is* ethical in the sense that it stresses God's requirement that justice be done in righteous ways. Thus, ethics is a reference point for prophets in anticipating transformation. This implies that morality must inform our efforts to transform both church and world.

In many respects, such an understanding of the prophetic vocation of the community of faith has invariably been neutralized. The established social-political-economic system has been the primary cause of this neutralization. In general, it is possible to find Christian communities that have not perceived or have simply remained unaffected by the overwhelming problems facing humanity. These communities lack understanding of the deep meaning of prophetic vocation.

The word "vocation" comes up in a variety of contexts. It has been used as a synonym for "profession," "talent," and "occupation." While such an idea can reveal a call that leads to conscious and committed action, it can also disclose alienating tendencies without any sensitivity to contextual realities. In this book, however, the conceptual sense of the term *vocatio* is to be understood as both theological and ethical. It is understood as the Christian response to God's call for the sake of the collective well-being of the family of God—God's kin-dom.[27] It is a call for socio-economic transformation that is rooted in Christian action and focused on the common good. Therefore, the term "vocation," as used here, is in conjunction with its prophetic dimension.

---

26. Heschel, *The Prophets*, 201.

27. Isasi-Diaz coined the "kin-dom," replacing the Bible's eschatological "kingdom of God." In her own words, there are two reasons for the rejection of the term "kingdom of God:" "There are two reasons for not using the regular word employed by English Bibles, *kingdom*. First, it is obviously a sexist word that presumes that God is male. Second, the concept of kingdom in our world today is both hierarchical and elitist—which is also why I do not use *reign*. The word *kin-dom* makes it clearer that when the fullness of God becomes a day-to-day reality in the world at large, we will all be sisters and brothers—kin to each other" (see Isasi-Diaz, "Solidarity: Love of Neighbor in the 1980s," 304n4).

PROPHETIC TEACHINGS AND THE PRAXIS OF JESUS

Another conceptual reference to the prophetic praxis of the community of faith comes from Jesus Christ as the incarnate prophet. Even though Jesus does not clearly and explicitly claim himself as a prophet, it has been accepted that prophetic praxis is implicit in his sayings and actions.[28] One of the most common replies to the question, "Who is this Jesus?" is, "He is a prophet" (a prophet from the Hebrew tradition) as Luke testifies. Luke, recalling the words of the prophet Moses, reads as follows, "Moses said: 'The Lord your God will raise up for you from your own people a prophet like me. You must listen to whatever he tells you. And it will be that everyone who does not listen to that prophet will be utterly rooted out of the people.'" (Acts 3:22–23).

Jesus' message is filled with political, social, and economic connotations, which challenged the *status quo* of the Roman imperialistic period and the religious authorities of his time. Jesus' message was a threat to the political and social order precisely because his prophetic message challenged and demanded political and social change. As R. David Kaylor says: Jesus preached and taught a message that was thoroughly political, a message that demanded a social or political revolution . . . To claim that Jesus was "political" is to say that Jesus promoted a restoration of the covenant community on the basis of the Torah and the prophets, both of which regarded the mundane aspects of life as "spiritual" issues.[29]

At the very beginning of his public ministry, Jesus establishes his "political platform" by announcing his preferential option for the poor, using the words of the prophet Isaiah, saying, "The Spirit of the Lord is upon me, because he has anointed me to bring good news to the poor. He has sent me to proclaim release to the captives and recovery of sight to the blind, to let the oppressed go free, to proclaim the year of the Lord's favor" (Luke 4:17–19). Jesus' inaugural address effectively defined his prophetic platform. Jesus declares the time of the fulfillment of God's promises. It is the time where God's grace and favor will encounter the poor, the captives, the blind, and the oppressed. Julio de Santa Ana interprets this passage as follows: "This text emphasized what we might call the privilege of the poor. In adding after this passage from Isaiah, 'Today this scripture has

---

28. Aune, *Prophecy in Early Christianity*, 153.

29. Kaylor, *Jesus the Prophet*, 3–4. As quoted by Herzog in *Jesus, Justice, and the Reign of God*, 63.

been fulfilled in your hearing' (Luke 4:21), Jesus identifies himself as the messenger proclaimed by the prophet and, at the time, explains that his mission is addressed to the unfortunate, the poor, to whom He already announces an end to their sufferings. Their special place is confirmed by the beatitudes . . . In these texts Jesus indicates that with his coming the poor will be blessed, 'for theirs is the Kingdom of heaven.'"[30] Jesus' prophetic word is addressed to the ones less favored by the society of his time. These people know what it is like to be oppressed. The Roman occupiers were the oppressors, the controllers, and invaders of the land promised to them. The prophetic voice of Jesus speaks directly to them, saying that their time of oppression is over.

Jesus did not make distinctions between classes of human beings. Rather, he treated all people as equals. Jesus also did not treat people differently according to their socio-economic status, their education, their gender, their age, their ethnicity, or their sexual preferences. Instead, he listened to them; he ate at the same table with them; he visited them; he taught them; he touched them; he forgave them, and he healed them. Jesus' prophetic mission was to show how God does not exclude anyone, and to teach how to break down the barriers that separate people from living in common as in a pleasant garden.[31]

One clear implication of all that we hear, read, and learn from Jesus' prophetic praxis was that his ministry is incontestably immersed into the social, political, and economic agenda of his time. Jesus, the incarnated prophet, did not support any exclusion, oppression, or injustice against any human being. His preference for prophetic praxis was rooted in the Torah. His pedagogical strategy was rooted in the parables. As William Herzog says, "Jesus proposed a prophetic reading of the Torah that critiqued injustice and appealed to another order, the reign of God. The parables were part

---

30. Santa Ana, *Good News to the Poor*, 13.

31. Alves, in the chapter "Prophecy" of his book *The Poet, The Warrior, The Prophet*, plays magisterially with the concept of garden as a metaphor of human existence. As I understand it, we are all called to be prophets-gardeners. He says: "We were born in a garden, there is a garden inside our bodies, and we are destined by divine vocation to be gardeners, because God also is a gardener. God was not happy in the infinity of the universe. His work moves from the boundless lifeless spaces of the universe to this little, circumscribed space, where life makes love with beauty. In the garden his work is finished. In the garden he finds pleasure. He rests from work. He becomes, then, pure contemplation, pure play, pure enjoyment. Nothing else is to be done. No ethics, no commandment, no politics: there is a fruit to be eaten" (see Alves, *The Poet, the Warrior, the Prophet*, 129).

of that larger strategy, which included a prophetic critique of the systems of oppression and of the ruling class and proposals for prophetic action."[32] Herzog continues, "Jesus' ministry was concerned with political and economic issues. Matters of justice were not peripheral to a spiritual gospel but were at the heart of his proclamation and praxis. Perhaps it would be more accurate to say that justice was at the center of Jesus' spirituality."[33] Jesus' spirituality is an active and disturbing one. When we admit that Jesus' spirituality is prophetic, we open the possibility of having our own spiritual comfort threatened. This can be most disturbing. Jesus' prophetic spirituality is incompatible with spiritual alienation. To follow Jesus is to walk through his uncomfortable zone of breaking the barriers of human segregation. When we admit that Jesus is a prophet, we must walk in his footsteps toward the needy, breaking down the arrogance of indifference to the suffering in the world. As Heschel reminds us, indifference to social evil and injustice is among the greatest evil in the sight of God and the prophet. "Indifference to evil is more insidious than evil itself."[34]

From this brief overview of the prophetic praxis of Jesus, I turn now to the witness of those who, in the history of the Church, are considered the pillars who have sustained the prophetic voice committed to social-political-economic transformation in society.

EARLY CHRISTIAN APOLOGISTS

An early contribution comes from Justin Martyr (100–165) who wrote his *Apology* in defense of Christianity that was addressed to the Roman emperor Antoninus Pius in the middle of the second century. The following excerpt, from 1 *Apology* 67, represents, among other things, Justin's description of a Eucharistic service with considerable concern and care for those in need. Justin says:

> Those who have the means help all those who are in want, and we continually meet together. And over all that we take to eat we bless the creator of all things through God's Son Jesus Christ and the Holy Spirit . . . There is a distribution of the things over which thanks have been said and each person participates, and these things are sent by the deacons to those who are not present. Those

32. Herzog, *Parables as Subversive Speech*, 264.

33. Ibid.

34. Heschel, *The Prophets*, 2:64. See also Heschel, *The Insecurity of Freedom*, 92.

who are prosperous and who desire to do so, give what they wish, according to each one's own choice, and the collection is deposited with the presider. He aids orphans and widows, those who are in want through disease or through another cause, those who are in prison, and foreigners who are sojourning here. In short, the presider is a guardian to all those who are in need.[35]

Justin's sacramental sensitivity and prophetic consciousness attest his commitment to the well being of everyone. For him, the distribution of the "things over which thanks have been said" is a sign of love and care that goes beyond the Eucharistic ritual itself. Justin's eyes, ears, and hands are open to the ones in need: orphans and widows, the sick and those who are in want, the prisoners and the foreigners. In sum, as Justin said about the presider, we can be assured that we are all guardians to all those who are in need.

Another contribution comes from John Chrysostom, Bishop of Constantinople (347–407), who, because of his eloquence was called the "golden mouthed" one. Chrysostom called the church's attention to the need to remain alert to acknowledging Christ's presence whenever the poor, the hungry, the naked, the homeless, the thirsty, the prisoners, and many others despised by society, are served. Here is his thought:

> The master and creator of the universe says, "I was hungry and you gave me no food" (Matt 25:42). What heart is so hard that it is not moved by these words? Your Lord is out there, dying of hunger, and you give yourself up to gluttony. And the terrible thing is not only this, but as you give yourself up to gluttony, you calmly despise him, and it is very little He asks of you: a piece of bread to assuage his hunger. He is out there, dying of cold, and you dress yourself in silk and turn your gaze away from him, showing him no compassion, but go on your way without mercy. What pardon can such action merit? Then let us not devote our efforts to accumulating wealth at all cost. Let us also consider the way of administering it properly and helping the needy; and let us not exaggerate in the goods which remain and cannot be transferred. This is why the Lord has hidden the last day from us; He wants us to remain alert and vigilant, to encourage us to virtue: "Watch, therefore, for you know neither the day nor the hour." (Matt 25:13)[36]

---

35. As quoted in Lathrop, *Holy Things*, 45.
36. As quoted by Santa Ana, *Good News to the Poor*, 19–20.

Chrysostom's words and prophetic vision are still current. It is striking that he can see Christ "out there, dying of hunger," "despised," "dying of cold," in the life and in the human condition of so many in the world. His political-economic vision is also current and as strong as the prophet's committed militancy: "let us not devote our efforts to accumulating wealth at all cost." As Christians, we are challenged to see Christ in the needy, the hungry, the oppressed, the marginalized, and the disenfranchised. Chrysostom's commentary on Acts 4:32–35 is also noteworthy. He writes:

> Charity makes you see another self in your neighbor, and teaches you to rejoice in his goods as in your own, to tolerate his defects as your own. Charity makes one body of all, and of their souls, in which the Holy Spirit dwells. And thus the Spirit of peace does not rest on the separated, but on those whose souls are united. Charity makes what each owns the property of all, as is shown in the book of Acts.[37]

Here, Chrysostom stresses brotherly charity as an element of communal responsibility towards the unity of the Body of Christ. The ability to see "another self in your neighbor" and "to rejoice in his goods as in your own, to tolerate his defects as your own," are gifts and virtues of those with prophetic consciousness.

Ambrose (340–397), Bishop of Milan from 374 to 397, stressed the idea that to follow Christ is to conform to what Christ has done for others. According to Ambrose:

> If anyone seeks to please everyone, let him seek what is useful to many and not only to himself, following the example of St. Paul. This is what it means to conform oneself to Christ, not desiring what is improper and not harming another to benefit oneself. Our Lord Jesus Christ, being God, humbled himself and took the form of man (Phil 2:6–7), which he enriched with the virtues of his works. Would you dare to deprive those whom Christ protected, or neglect those whom Christ clothed? For this is what you do when you put your own interest before another's.[38]

A prophetic mind considers "what is useful to many and not only to himself." Ambrose's social spirit and sensitivity led him to see others' need as fundamental for the establishment of a just life for all, not just for some.

37. Ibid., 41.
38. Ibid., 46.

Christian ethics implies putting others' interests before own. The market and the business world call for a different approach today.

The Shepherd of Hermas (first or second century), called for solidarity and charity. Julio de Santa Ana argues that the Shepherd of Hermas, "sees in the lack of solidarity with the humble a sign of unfaithfulness to the Lord who calls us to live in brotherly love."[39] We find the following contribution of the Shepherd of Hermas:

> To those who can do good, tell them to continue doing so, for it is beneficial for them to do good works. For my part, I want them to know that every man must be free from his needs. For he who is in need and poverty in his daily life is in great torment and anxiety. Thus he who frees the soul of such a man from his need attains great joy for himself. He who suffers such calamity undergoes the same torment and torture as a man in prison. The fact is that many, unable to bear such misfortune, take their own lives. Hence he who knows the suffering of such a man and does not free him from it commits a grave sin and is guilty of his blood.[40]

Here is another example of a great Christian prophetic voice. What is at stake here is the compassion and love for those in need—a social virtue. The opposition of it would be "social sin." Expanding the Shepherd of Hermas' theological approach, we can conjecture the concept of "social sin" as all social structures that compromise human dignity. They cause people to suffer oppression, discrimination, injustice, and so many other anti-life human conditions and are indeed "social sins" that do not free humans from their needs.

Yet another contribution from the early Church writers comes from Basil the Great (329–379), Bishop of Caesarea. Basil saw the irresponsible accumulation of wealth by private individuals as a sign of iniquity, negligent economic growth, and serious disrespect for the poor and the needy. He wrote:

> Indeed, you who will die some day, what are you thinking? "I will pull down my barns, and build larger ones." You do well, I say in turn: your barns of iniquity deserve to be demolished. Destroy with your own hands what you have built for this evil purpose. Pull down those storerooms which have never helped anyone. Destroy this house where you keep the fruits of your avarice, demolish

---

39. Ibid., 55.
40. Ibid.

those roofs, bring down those walls, put the harvest wheat on the ground, free your wealth from the prison in which you have kept it, and let light shine into the shadowy caves of your fortune. "I will pull down my barns, and build larger ones." And when these are full too, what do you think you will do? Destroy them again and build more new ones? What could be more foolish forever tiring yourself out, carefully building barns only to pull them down again? If you like, your barns could very well serve to house the poor. So harvest your treasure in heaven.[41]

Those who accumulate, and "have never helped anyone," have built for evil purpose, says Basil. Accumulation promotes inequality and unfair distribution of wealth, which has disastrous consequences for the poor and excluded to extreme level.

Ambrose offered a thought about this that parallels Basil's. Since Ambrose seems to amplify Basil's contribution, I include his contribution here.

Do you hear, rich man, what the Lord says? You come to the church not to distribute anything to the poor but to take something away from them; you fast, not so that the cost of your meal may benefit the poor, but in order to seize all that he has. What pretence are you making with the book, the letters, the seal, the notes, the link with the law? Have you not heard? "Break all the fetters of injustice, unfasten the bonds that oppress, let the oppressed go free, and break the evil yoke." You offer me the tablets on which the law is inscribed, but I propose to you the law of God; you write with ink, but I repeat to you the oracles of the prophets, written under the inspiration of God; you prepare false witness, I ask for the witness of conscience, from whose judgment you can neither escape nor free yourself, whose witness you cannot refute in the day when God reveals the hidden world of men. You say: "I will pull down my barns" (Luke 12:18); but God says: "Rather give up what is enclosed in your barns, give it to the poor, so that the needy may make use of these resources." You say: "I will make them bigger, and use them to store my harvest, however abundant they are." But the Lord says to you: "Share your bread with the hungry." You say: "I will take the poor men's houses from them." But the Lord says to you: "Welcome to your house the needy who have no roof over their heads." Rich man, why do you think God will listen to you if you do not think you need to listen to God?"[42]

41. Ibid., 69.
42. Ibid., 103–4.

The context presented by Basil and Ambrose makes us wonder that neo-liberalism is not restrained to this era. To keep "the fruit of [ones] avarice," as Basil said and "give up what is enclosed in your barns, give it to the poor, so that the needy may make use of these resources," as resoundingly said by Ambrose, are ways to say that economic accumulation and unfair distribution are sins on a grand scale. As prophets, we are called to read the signs of the times.

The last contribution I will cite comes from Augustine (354–430), Bishop of Hippo. In his *Commentary of the Psalms*, he presents a remarkable declaration for justice and peace. Introducing Augustine's commentary on Psalms 85, Santa Ana says, "Indeed, without equality between the different sectors of society, social tensions cannot be overcome; antagonisms and contradictions tend to become more acute. Justice becomes a condition for peace, and when the distance between social groups tends to diminish, the possibilities of confrontation and conflict also decrease."[43] In his commentary on Psalms 85 Augustine wrote:

> Mercy and truth came together; justice and peace embraced each other. Do justice and you will have peace, so that justice and peace may embrace. If you do not love justice you will not have peace, for the two love and embrace each other. He who does justice finds peace; peace embraces justice. They are friends. Perhaps you love one and not the other, for there is no one who does not love peace, but not everyone wants to act justly. If you ask all men, "Do you love peace?" all the human race answers together, "I love it, I desire it, I long for it." Therefore, they must love justice, for they are friends and embrace each other. If you do not love the friend of peace, it will not love you and will not come to you. Do you think it is a great thing to desire peace? Any perverse man desires it. Well, it is a good thing, peace. But do justice, for justice and peace embrace each other and do not fight.[44]

Augustine's commitment to Christian praxis of justice, love and peace echoes all prophetic actions throughout the biblical prophetic messages. The cry for justice and peace is an in heritance from the prophets. Every prophetic praxis has to have an equivalent gesture of love, of justice, of service, of hospitality, of solidarity, of peace, and ultimately of life for all.

---

43. Ibid., 104.
44. Ibid., 104–5.

These ancient Christian prophetic voices set the tone for the development of critical analysis of reality in the contemporary scene. Is it not true that all of these ancient Christian words still resonate and shake our consciousness today? This is what prophetic voices are all about. The community that understands and lives the prophetic dimension of the liturgy is called and challenged to shake human animosity, apathy and impotence before the signs of evil, death, and injustice that corrode the sense of human dignity.

CONTEMPORARY PROPHETIC PRAXIS

Prophetic praxis is the actuality of Christ's ministry in our midst: healing our loss of sight to the unwillingness to look at all of God's people as our neighbors; releasing us from captivity to rigid rules and structures that favor and protect our own comfort; and setting us free from selfish interests that keep us far from God, from our neighbor, from ourselves, and from longing for the desire for the possibility that justice and peace might embrace each other.

One of the possible ways to explore prophetic praxis is through critical Christian consciousness, commitment and praxis. An important instrument to develop such a critical consciousness is the *see-judge-act* method, also known as the hermeneutic circle.[45] This method brings light to the

45. The hermeneutic circle has its foundation in the "see-judge-act" method. This methodology has its incipient development in Thomas Aquinas (*Summa Theologica, Treatise On Prudence and Justice*, IIa IIae q. 47 a. 8) and most recently was appropriated by Catholic Action, led by Joseph Cardijn, and also as a tool for social-political-ideological analysis applied by liberation theology. Vásquez helps us understand the method. He says: "The see-judge-act method was introduced in the late 1940s by Joseph Cardijn, one of the central figures in the development of Catholic Action. Intent on reaching the laity in their homes and workplaces, Cardijn developed the see-judge-act method to understand the particular life conditions of the various segments of the emerging working class. The method is in essence a dynamic process of reflection and action. It departs from a specific social fact, seeking to identify the economic, social, political and ideological conditions that lie behind that fact. It then moves to a second moment in which the fact is analyzed and evaluated to ascertain whether it violates ideals of justice and solidarity. If it does, then the question arises: what courses of action can be taken to change the situation so that it would be more compatible with the Christian vision of the world? On the basis of this reflection the individuals engaged in this pedagogical exercise can undertake an informed emancipator praxis. Praxis, in turn, leads to new problems and questions that can be taken up in a new 'see' moment, thereby initiating another cycle of reflection and action" (Vásquez, *The Brazilian Popular Church and the Crisis of*

social-political-economic analysis in the contemporary prophetic praxis. In the context of Latin American liberation theology, the biblical passage from Exodus poses a direct connection to the essence of the hermeneutic circle, which resonates well in the contemporary prophetic ear. The text says: "Then the Lord said, 'I have *observed the misery* of my people who are in Egypt; I have *heard their cry* on account of their taskmasters. Indeed, I *know their sufferings,* and I have *come down to deliver them* from the Egyptians, and to bring them up out of that land to a good and broad land, a land flowing with milk and honey" (Exodus 3:7–8, emphasis added). The hermeneutical circle can be clearly observed in this passage: God "observed the misery" of God's people (see); evaluated and rationalized, "know their sufferings" (judge); and engaged in emancipator praxis, "come down to deliver them" (act).

On the basis of what has been said up to this point, I will next briefly consider contributions from authentic prophets of more contemporary times: Dom Hélder Câmara, Mother Teresa, Martin Luther King, Jr., and Archbishop Oscar Romero.

Dom Hélder Câmara (1909–1999), a Brazilian Roman Catholic archbishop, lived in flesh Christ's gospel of love, justice, and peace. It was in the year of 1964 that he became archbishop of Olinda and Recife—two challenging poor areas in Northeast Brazil. His famous phrase, "When I give food to the poor, they call me a saint. When I ask why the poor have no food, they call me a communist"[46] certainly helped him to become known as the "red bishop." Dom Hélder was not against progress; rather he advocated for a progress made in our minds and hearts. He claimed that the world progress would not be legitimate without social awareness, social conscience. He says:

> If I speak in the name of God and the poor
> I cannot be against progress.
> When I see how much the human mind
> has already invented and manufactured
> to deliver women and men from cold and hunger,
> from pain, sickness, and suffering,
> from ignorance, from isolation, and so on,
> I have to say: we must go on.
> There is still far too much hunger, pain,
> disease, ignorance, and solitude.

Modernity, 26–27).

46. *Dom Hélder Câmara: Essential Writings,* 11.

Human beings, God's co-creators,
still have a great deal to do to finish and perfect creation,
the mission they have received from the Lord.
And so I say to you:
let us walk courageously, daringly, along the road of progress.
But let us be careful not to crush anyone,
not to leave anyone lying in the ditch.
The progress we have to make first, then,
may not be in our super-laboratories and super-factories.
It may have to be made in our minds and hearts.
What I mean is that it will have to be made
in our appetite for and will to progress.
Progress for what? For what kind of growth? For whose profit?
There is no truly human progress
without progress in social awareness, social conscience.[47]

The prophet's mind is focused on what will benefit the least favored of society. His or her day-to-day effort is concentrated on making life better for everyone, not just for some. There are political implications for prophetic praxis. Dom Hélder's prophetic posture reveals a spiritual sensitivity in direct relation with social-political-economic consciousness. He says:

When two-thirds of humanity in the world
is in a state of underdevelopment,
how can large amounts of money be spent
in building temples of stone,
and Christ's living presence
in the person of the poor be forgotten?
Christ is surely there,
immersed in misery and hunger,
living in dilapidated huts
without health or job,
without prospects for a future.[48]

As a prophet of his time, he knew the social, political and economic contexts in which he built a theological perspective and social praxis that affirm the gospel message of loving God and the neighbor. Dom Hélder portrayed a Christian prophetic praxis committed to the well being of the larger community seeking social change for the benefit of all. His prophetic vision and

47. Dom Hélder Câmara's quote in Schipani and Wessels, *The Promise of Hope: A Tribute to Dom Hélder*, 22.

48. Ibid., xi.

legacy is recognized around the globe as one who lived a pilgrimage for peace and hope for a better tomorrow.

The next expressive contemporary prophetic voice I want to bring to our attention is Mother Teresa (1910–1997), also known as Mother Teresa of Calcutta, born in Skopje, the current capital of the Republic of Macedonia. She was baptized as Agnes Gonxha Bojaxhiu. As a Roman Catholic nun and missionary, Mother Teresa devoted her life to caring for the sick, the poor, the dying, and the little children. Her sensitivity to the sufferings of the poorest of the poor—marginalized by a savage economic system— and her persistent voice lifting up those rejected by society were signs of her unconditional commitment to love kindness and to walk humbly with God. Mother Teresa's life and work testify why the world recognized her as the "prophet of love."

Mother Teresa soon realized that if she had not worked on behalf of the poor and marginalized, they would not live with dignity. Their cries for help would not be heard and there would be no transformation in their lives. Her prophetic sensitivity, then, compelled her to establish a new order called Missionary of Charity. She described its mission as to care for "the hungry, the naked, the homeless, the crippled, the blind, the lepers, all those people who feel unwanted, unloved, uncared for throughout society, people that have become a burden to society and are shunned by everyone."[49] As prophet, Mother Teresa interpreted reality from God's perspective. She knew that in God's sight we are all God's children, each bestowed irreversible, nonnegotiable, human dignity. She knew that it is our task and duty to uphold and preserve this great human treasure. She says:

> When a poor person dies of hunger, it has not happened because God did not take care of him or her. It has happened because neither you nor I wanted to give that person what he or she needed. We have refused to be instruments of love in the hands of God to give the poor a piece of bread, to offer them a dress with which to ward off the cold. It has happened because we did not recognize Christ when, once more, he appeared under the guise of pain, identified with a man numb from the cold, dying of hunger, when he came in a lonely human being, in a lost child in search of a home.[50]

---

49. Mother Teresa's quote in Goll and Goll, *Compassion*, 122.
50. Teresa, *In My Own Words*, 16.

This passage reveals Mother Teresa's prophetic sensitivity in action. Her ability to see reality, to read and analyze its effects, and to act consciously seeking transformation reveals a prophetic praxis demonstrated only by a small and select courageous group of people.

Mother Teresa had the unusual capacity to love and to care for other human beings to the highest level—as an expression embodied in the Christian principle of "love your neighbor as yourself." Her life and ministry revealed that to love her neighbor as herself, to the ultimate level, meant seeing herself in the life of others, especially in the lives of the destitute, the afflicted, the hungry, the sick, and the poor—humanity in its spiritual essence. Archbishop Desmond Tutu explores this concept of humanity— the essence of being a human being—through the Bantu language term *ubuntu*. He says: "*Ubuntu* addresses a central tenet of African philosophy: the essence of what it is to be human."[51] The term invites us to reflect in the togetherness, the interdependence, and the sense of belonging, hospitality, generosity, and compassion as the essence of humanity. We are who we are through other human beings. I am because we are. Me and We goes inseparably together. This African concept helps us understand and value the other human being because he or she has parts of you and me in his or her life, and we have parts of his or her life in us.

Mother Teresa's prophetic life and ministry testify to the *ubuntu* as an integral part of her life—the essence of her humanity. Archbishop Tutu describes the *ubuntu* concept further when mentioning Mother Teresa's life. He says: "This is the essence of *ubuntu*, or 'me we,' and in this are reflected vividly the life and actions of Mother Theresa. Her entire being was focused on bringing some dignity and compassion into the lives of the destitute and the afflicted. In a world that is hard and cynical, she showed that great things can be achieved wherever there is great love, not only among the desperate of Calcutta but throughout the world. The *ubuntu* of Mother Theresa showed that the only way we can ever be human is together. The only way we can be free is together."[52] The world today needs to embrace this concept as Mother Teresa did. Her love for human beings, her passionate dedication to the well being of God's children, and her prophetic voice claiming justice for the poor are proclamations of human dignity and sources of inspiration for prophetic praxis seeking transformation in the Church and society today and for years to come.

51. Teresa, *Love: The Words and Inspiration of Mother Teresa*, 3.
52. Ibid., 5.

Another contemporary prophetic voice that still strongly resonates in our world today is that of Martin Luther King Jr. (1929–1968), a Baptist minister, known worldwide as a key leader of the US civil rights movement. He was widely known as a human being who was aware of the signs of his time and place. Martin Luther King Jr. was a minister, a theologian, a social ethicist, a prophet, with so many other attributes of one who offer his or her life for the well-being of all humans. As a minister, he preached the social gospel of Jesus Christ. Regarding King's approach to pastoral ministry, Rufus Burrow Jr. states: "King's ideal of the minister was one who is intellectually astute and invigorating, and one who strives to live by and apply the ethical ideals of the Jewish and Christian faiths to the social struggle."[53] As a theologian, King was deeply influenced by the social gospel and the philosophy of personalism.[54] As social ethicist, Martin Luther King built his conviction based on the fact that any theological studies, any philosophical understandings, any pastoral engagements would mean nothing if not applied to eradicate evil forces that violate human dignity. Burrow helps clarify the juxtaposition of King's theology of personalism and his socio-ethical convictions. Burrow writes: "The real questions for him [King] were: What does the dignity or sacredness of persons mean in the most concrete sense of day-to-day living for those with their backs pressed against the wall (to use a phrase coined by Howard Thurman), that is, those among the disinherited? What does the conviction that God is personal mean concretely for those victimized by racism as well as for those who benefit from it? What will such personalistic convictions look like once they have been applied to the struggle for freedom and justice?"[55] These are foundational questions for prophetic praxis. The Church needs to hear King's prophetic voice and stand with him in scrutinizing every segment of society. King says: "The Church must forever stand in judgment upon every political, social and economic system, condemning evil wherever they exist."[56] For King, philosophy, theology and pastoral praxis are interrelated and need to find their ultimate meaning in dialogue with the concrete, savage world.

Abraham Joshua Heschel once said about King: "Where in America today do we hear a voice like the voice of the prophets of Israel? Martin

---

53. Burrow, *Martin Luther King, Jr. for Armchair Theologians*, 44.

54. For further study on King's theological, philosophical, and ethical principles, see Burrow, *God and Human Dignity*, 2006.

55. Burrow, *God and Human Dignity*, 69–70.

56. As quoted by Burrow, *Martin Luther King, Jr. for Armchair Theologians*, 165.

Luther King is a sign that God has not forsaken the United States of America. God has sent him to us. His presence is the hope of America. His mission is sacred, his leadership of supreme importance to every one of us . . . I call upon every Jew to harken to his voice, to share his vision, to follow in his way. The whole future of America will depend upon the impact and influence of Dr. King."[57] The world, not just the United States, has a tremendous prophetic example to follow—a faithful disciple of Christ whose dream and prophetic voice has radically shaken the *status quo*. Here are excerpts of his "I Have a Dream" speech:

> And so even though we face the difficulties of today and tomorrow, I still have a dream. It is a dream deeply rooted in the American Dream.
>
> I have a dream that one day this nation will rise up and live out the true meaning of its creed: We hold these truths to be self-evident, that all men are created equal.
>
> I have a dream that one day on the red hills of Georgia the sons of former slaves and the sons of former slave owners will be able to sit down together at the table of brotherhood.
>
> I have a dream that one day even the state of Mississippi, a state sweltering with the heat of injustice, sweltering with the heat of oppression, will be transformed into an oasis of freedom and justice.
>
> II have a dream that my four little children will one day live in a nation where they will not be judged by the color of their skin but by the content of their character. I have a dream today![58]

Let humanity not forget Martin Luther King's dream, nor forget his prophetic legacy.

It has been said, and it will be emphasized throughout this book, that the spirit of a prophet has his or her ears open to God and the eyes focused on the contextual reality of life. The prophet sees, hears, and feels what happens around him or her, and speak up with fire in his or her mouth. As prophet, King's ears were open to God, his eyes focused on the contextual reality of his time, and his feet tirelessly marched towards freedom, against war, for human rights. His ears did not close to the cries of the needy claiming justice; his eyes did not close to the continuing problem of racial discrimination and segregation; and his feet did not stop marching sta for

57. Heschel and Heschel. *Abraham Joshua Heschel: Essential Writings*, 84.

58. Echols, *I Have a Dream*, 7.

righteousness, for truth, for peace, and for equal rights. Martin Luther King Jr.'s legacy is a gift from God to humanity. He was a prophet of our time.

The last contemporary prophetic presence I want to cite is that of Archbishop Romero. Oscar Arnulfo Romero (1917–1980) from El Salvador is recognized as the Salvadoran martyr, prophet, and apostle of social-political-economic justice for the poor. Oscar Romero was acclaimed as saint by the *campesinos* and victims of the military, the government, and the land oligarchy in El Salvador. He was also acclaimed as "a *pastor* who defended his people, a *prophet* who confronted the enemies of the people, and a *martyr*, faithful to the end to the God who sent him to save the people."[59] It is important to note that the "people" of whom Archbishop Romero speaks are the ones he loved and to whom he offered his own life—his brothers and sisters: the poor. In his homily of July 15, 1979, he said:

> I am glad, brothers and sisters,
> that our church is persecuted
> precisely for its preferential option for the poor
> and for trying to become incarnate
> on behalf of the poor.
> And I want to say to all the people,
> to rulers,
> to the rich and powerful:
> If you do not become poor,
> if you do not concern yourselves
> for the poverty of our people
> as though they were your own family,
> you will not be able to save society.[60]

His love for the poor—"the people" as frequently expressed in his homilies—manifested his tireless prophetic denunciation of the critical life lived by his beloved ones. In his homily of July 24, 1979, he fervently expressed: "I will not tire of denouncing abuse by arbitrary arrests, by disappearances, by torture."[61] Like Jesus, Archbishop Romero was deeply moved by the sufferings of the people. As prophet, he denounced and judged the social-political-economic systems of his context from God's perspective—God's prophetic will. As Jon Sobrino says, "the political, the economic, and the social are consubstantial with history, and thus constitute the object of

59. Sobrino, *No Salvation Outside the Poor*, 121–22.
60. Brockman, *The Church Is All of You*, 90.
61. Sobrino, *No Salvation Outside the Poor*, 111.

God's prophetic will."[62] There is no other way for prophetic praxis without considering it from the perspective of God's will to the people. God's prophetic will was the source and motivation of Archbishop Romero's prophetic praxis. In his homily of January 21, 1979, Archbishop Romero said: "I must insist that my sermons are not political. Naturally, they deal with the political. They deal with the reality of the lives of the people. But they do so in order to enlighten the people, and to tell them what is the will of God and what is not the will of God."[63] His primary focus was to show God to his people, so they could find strength for liberation, and that was his final gift to the community: he was murdered while presiding over the Eucharist.

These ancient and contemporary prophetic examples presented above are sources of inspiration for prophetic praxis. Immersed in their prophetic vocation, we saw glimpses of their call to be means of transformation in the church and in the world. As prophets, they explored their capacity to read reality, to evaluate its effects, and to act consciously in the historical context where they lived, in the world. All the above examples confirm the conviction that prophetic praxis mediates God's grace, love, favor and blessings. When we reach this ideal level of prophetic praxis—as mediation of God's grace—we engage ourselves in a transforming, even "sacramental" experience. The sacrament as prophetic voice is the subject of the next chapter.

---

62. Sobrino, *Archbishop Romero*, 104.

63. Ibid.

2

Sacrament as Prophetic Voice

THE STUDY OF GRAMMAR teaches us that an adjective modifies or qualifies the meaning of a noun or phrase. To understand the use of the adjective "prophetic" in this study, one must understand the context in which it is being applied. The context communicates its profound meaning; interpretation is needed in order to understand what has been communicated. Thus, to engage in a more specific discussion about sacrament as prophetic voice, we need to not only understand the adjective "prophetic," which was already discussed in the previous chapter, but we also need to understand another adjective related to the task of prophecy: "sacramental." The adjective, "sacramental," points to a transcendent symbolic reality that goes beyond the common understanding of its meaning.

The interpreter assimilates the nature of "sacramental" when he or she, even a community as a whole, is directly and cognitively connected with the symbolic reality making possible the use of the term. Terms such as "sacramental theology," "sacramental rites," "sacramental worship," "sacramental understanding," "sacramental community," "sacramental life," and even "sacramental prophetic voice" present different realities, each one with its own peculiar applicability in theological, liturgical, and ritual senses. In other words, the adjective "sacramental" points beyond the logic of what characterizes its own root—the term "sacrament." It has the dynamic connotation of a living sacred experience in which a person or a community engages in transcendent reality. Dwight Vogel, in his book *Food for Pilgrims: A Journey with Saint Luke*, develops this idea in a helpful way. He writes that, "When we say something is sacramental, we are saying that it is an unusually transparent experience which reveals a reality which is much deeper behind it. It is symbolic in the profound sense of that word."[1] A sacramental experience reveals a transcendent, divine reality. It takes us into an experience of God in which we truly encounter the divine; we are called into a deeper relationship with God.

The understanding of prophetic voice as sacramental is deeply related to the transcendent symbolic reality present in a given action, be it written or experienced. The unusually translucent[2] and deeper reality behind the prophetic action brings to it the sacramental dimension; a dimension which recurs throughout an engaged, conscious, and committed Christian praxis of love, mercy, and justice. Sacramental celebration, grounded in this assumption, becomes the well that overflows with Christian prophetic praxis. Another way that extends our understanding and challenges our praxis is to explore the prophetic voice as sacramental.

A second insight, extending the meaning of sacrament as prophetic voice, comes from a simple statement presented by Kathleen Norris in her book *The Cloister Walk*. According to Norris, "Anyone with a sacramental understanding of the world knows that it's the small things that count."[3] This seems to be a modest statement with little connection with the main issues presented here, but if it is considered through the lens of a living sacramental "prophetic" spirituality, it has a deep and powerful meaning. This statement presents a deep awareness of an intense religious praxis that has the power of transformation. Even small acts make a difference in a religious sense. When sacramental understanding is expressed through "small things," transformation can occur. In order to capture the symbolic meaning of those "small things," we need to give life to the hidden desire of our religious sensibility. In considering the prophetic voice embodied in sacramental celebration, we will discover that what happens is precisely a result of simple facts, "small things," which establish tremendous impact of

---

1. Vogel, *Food for Pilgrims*, 6.

2. Regarding the expression "transparent experience" present in Vogel's quotation above, he would now prefer to use the expression "translucent experience." He argues that "translucent" brings a different perspective, a more disclosing and reflecting experience that reveals transcendent reality. In his most recent book, co-authored with Linda J. Vogel, we can find it clearly. They say: "When we say times and seasons can be sacramental, we mean they can become *unusually translucent experiences that open us to experiencing God*" (see Vogel and Vogel, *Syncopated Grace*, 21).

3. Norris, *The Cloister Walk*, 376.

the sacramental praxis of the Church. Accordingly, ordinary ritual events can become an extraordinary prophetic means of transformation. What we need is a sacramental understanding to live deeply the prophetic reality of the sacraments.

A third insight comes from the understanding that we can experience our beliefs through symbolic medium or sacred symbols; through something that when we see, smell, taste, touch, hear, or even imagine it, we experience a "magic" moment causing us appropriate a memorable spiritual time in our life as a sacred moment. For example, when we bring to our mind "a thing," an object, even a moment, which has symbolic meaning for us, something that has a special story, we can say that this symbolic medium has meaningful narrative—a sacramental significance.[4] They are means of sacred grace.

Here is one of my sacred stories. I have a silver table fork that I preserve with love and care in my home. As an object, it can be described from at least two different perspectives. First, we can focus on the product itself and the nature of its material. Is it made of silver, gold, iron, wood, plastic, etc? Similarly, we can focus on its *market value*—its cost, how long it takes to be produced, and so on. Therefore, as an object, my table fork is similar to any other object in the world except for one thing: it was my beloved mom who gave it to me when I left home many years ago. This brings us to a second perspective: its symbolic meaning. The reality surrounding its existence makes it a very special symbol. It was a *gift*, and thus has deep symbolic significance. For me, it is not just a table fork anymore. As a *gift*, it speaks many silent, secret, and sacred things. It carries my mom's presence as I see, touch, use and take care of this special table fork. In this sense, I can say it has a sacramental meaning in it. It has a different meaning, a symbolic meaning pointing to a different reality. That is, there is means of grace carried by it because I know my mom is always praying to God, that all of her children and all families around the world may have food on their table. Its value transcends the object itself. As Leonardo Boff affirms, "The sacramental structure emerges when things begin to speak and human beings begin to hear their voices."[5] In other words, in the sacramental realm we need symbols. A thing becomes a symbol when we need to explain its

4. I am indebted here to Leonardo Boff, Rubem Alves, and Dwight Vogel and Linda Vogel who taught me to see, through their writings and lives, the symbolic sacramental meaning of life in its deepest level. See Boff, *Sacraments of Life*; Alves, *I Believe in the Resurrection of the Body*; Vogel and Vogel, *Sacramental Living*.

5. Boff, *Sacraments of Life, Life of the Sacraments*, 2.

mystery, to share its narrative because it communicates multiple levels of meaning. My table fork is, in fact, a sacramental gift. As such, the logic that sustains my relationship to it is a transcendental one, which is the logic of abundance graciousness. I treasure this table fork as an immeasurable value bringing translucent sacred reality of transcendent experience. This story reflects my personal assumption of sacramental understanding being born out of daily life experiences, which bring to human beings a passionate way to live and to make life in the world, created and sustained by the One who makes life a gift for all. Leonardo Boff expands on and further clarifies this sacramental understanding. He writes:

> Sacramental thinking means that the roads we travel, the mountains we see, the rivers that bathe our lands, the houses that inhabit our neighborhoods, and the persons that create our society, are not simply people, houses, rivers, mountains and roads like all the others in the world. They are unique and incomparable. They are a part of ourselves. So we rejoice and suffer over their fate. We lament the felling of the huge tree in our town square or the demolition of an old shed. Something of ourselves dies along with them. Why? Because they are no longer merely things. They are sacraments in our life.[6]

Dwight Vogel and Linda Vogel share a similar understanding. "Planting our roots, being connected with our own place and space, and being attuned to others' place and space," they write, "are spiritual disciplines which foster sacramental living."[7] My own understanding is that the reference to sacramental living is to be able to understand God-language in every aspect of our lives in which we experience remembrance, give thanks, and share with others. There are connections, alliances, recognitions, and remembrances. In sum, there is identification between giver and receiver. Theologically it now becomes possible to say that there is *grace*.

This chapter is concerned with sacrament as a means of spiritual growth in a bipartite dimension: a sacred pilgrimage hand in hand with God on one side, and with our neighbor on the other side. The focus, therefore, assumes that the spiritual intensity in serving our God connects directly to the prophetic passion of serving others in love, mercy, and justice. Service and mission are two necessary elements of a prophetic faith. With a prophetic perspective, the service due to God calls us to do mission—to

6. Ibid., 18.
7. Vogel and Vogel, *Sacramental Living*, 41.

be co-participants in the *Missio Dei*.[8] In essence, the sacraments, for the purpose of this work perceived through both Baptism and Eucharist, are the starting point for Christian prophetic praxis towards transformation.[9]

SACRAMENT: MEANING AND PRAXIS

What possible meanings can we infer from the word "sacrament?" How does the Christian community conceive these meanings and practice them in the plenitude of their significance? It is generally accepted that a sacrament is a religious act, rite, ceremony, or practice which is conceived as especially sacred. It is generally conceived as the outward sign of the inward grace of God. Theologians, throughout Christian history, have made significant contributions to the understanding of sacrament. For Christians of today and those of centuries past, trying to understand the mystery of the sacraments is an on-going theological challenge. In Christian tradition there are classical and foundational descriptions of sacrament that help delineate the concept. Louis-Marie Chauvet, for instance, summarizes some of these classical theological concepts as follows:

> *Augustine*
> The sacrament is the visible sacrifice of the invisible sacrifice, that is, a sacred sign. There is a sacrament in any celebration where the commemoration of the thing done is done in such a way as to be understood as signifying something to be received in a holy manner.

> *Isidore of Seville*
> The sacraments are so called because, under the veil of the visible [corporeal] things, the divine power works salvation [through these same sacraments] in a secret manner; hence, they are called sacraments owing to both their secret and sacred powers.

---

8. For a comprehensive approach to the concept of *Missio Dei*, see Bosch, *Transforming Mission*.

9. Dalmais supports the idea of celebrating worship in such a way that goes beyond the service due to God. He says, "The Church's liturgy has for its function, then, not only to offer God the worship due to him [*sic*] but also to make this mystery of salvation present and active among human being." This conception is vital for liturgical practice that enables the Church toward an active work of transformation in our society. See Dalmais, "The Liturgy as Celebration," in *Primary Sources of Liturgical Theology*, ed. Vogel, 25–26. For a complete edition, see Dalmais, "The Liturgy as Celebration," in *The Church at Prayer*, ed. Martimort and trans. O'Connell.

Paschasius Radbertus
A sacrament is something in any divine celebration which is given us as a pledge of salvation, when the thing visibly done effects, far inside, something other and invisible which must be received in a holy manner.

Peter Lombard
The sacrament bears the likeness of the thing of which it is the sign ... The sacrament indeed is properly so called because it is the sign of God's grace and the form of the invisible grace, so that it bears its image and stands as its cause.

Peter Abelard
The sacrament is the visible form of the invisible grace or the sign of a holy thing, that is, of something secret.[10]

As it is possible to perceive in these classical Roman Catholic theological concepts, sacrament is constituted by invisible grace through visible signs. The Fathers of the Church, as well as the Scholastics, developed their concept from the Latin *sacramentum, which was used to translate the Greek mysterion. Sacramentum, in the Roman law, was meant to be a pledge or an oath by which soldiers were bound.* The word was used to suggest something sacred and mysterious in virtue of Divine institution (*ex opere operato*). *Ex opere operato*,[11] that is, by virtue of the action, directs the *efficacy* of the action of the sacraments to the will of God as expressed by Christ's institution and promise. In this sense the expression *ex opere operato* suggests that the *efficacy* of the action does not depend upon anything human. In Thomas Aquinas' account, we see a short but emphatic definition for sacrament: "The sign of a sacred thing in so far as it sanctifies men" (*Signum rei sacrae in quantum est sanctificans hominess*).[12]

From the perspective of the Reformation period, the definition of sacrament brings a cluster of different theological approaches. Rubem Alves, a Brazilian protestant theologian, once said, "When things awaken longing remembrance and cause the memory of love and the desire for return to grow in the heart, we say that they are *sacraments*. This is a sacrament: visible signs of an absence, symbols which make us think about return."[13] In Alves' understanding, its mystery is the presence of an absence—clearly,

10. Chauvet, *Symbol and Sacrament*, 12–14.
11. See *The Catholic Encyclopedia*, s.v. "Sacraments."
12. Ibid., 296.
13. Alves, *I Believe in the Resurrection of the Body*, 14.

a protestant approach. James White helps summarizing as he quotes some Protestant perspectives, including:

> *Martin Luther*
> Sacraments are signs and testimonies of the will of God toward us; Sacraments are not merely . . . marks of profession among men.

> *Ulrich Zwingli*
> A sacrament is nothing else than an initiatory ceremony or a pledging;
> The sacraments are signs or ceremonials . . . by which a man proves to the Church that he either aims to be, or is, a soldier of Christ, and which inform the whole Church rather than yourself or your faith.

> *John Calvin*
> Sacrament is an outward sign by which the Lord seals on our consciences the promises of his good will toward us in order to sustain the weakness of our faith; and we in turn attest our piety toward him in the presence of the Lord and of his angels and before men; The sacraments offer and set forth Christ to us.[14]

Even though these quotations represent only a partial idea of what constitutes their understanding of the subject, these brief glimpses tell us the diverse theological approach among the reformers. The difference between Protestant and Roman Catholic approaches to the theological understanding of sacrament is that for the latter, sacrament *causes* and *effects* grace in the souls of the recipients, and for the former, sacraments are signs and means of grace.

Ole Borgen, in his book *John Wesley on the Sacraments*, states that John Wesley[15] adopts the Augustinian concept expressed in the Church of England Catechism. Borgen quotes Wesley on the subject, saying: "Our own Church . . . teaches us, that a sacrament is an outward sign of inward

---

14. White, *Sacraments as God's Self-Giving*, 17–20.

15. In order to understand John Wesley's sacramental theology, it would be appropriate to research the following Wesleyan primary sources: The *Sermons*, mainly "The Duty of Constant Communion," and "The Means of Grace;" the *Treatise on Baptism*; the *Journals*; the *Letters*; the *Notes upon the Old Testament* and *Notes upon the New Testament*; *A Roman Catechism*; the *Twenty-four Articles*; and the *Sunday Service of the Methodists in North America*. According to Borgen, these sources have considerable material relevant to the Wesleyan perspective on sacramental theology. See Borgen, *John Wesley on the Sacraments*, 20–36.

grace, and a means whereby we receive the same."[16] "Means of grace" is the central concept in Wesley's theology of the sacraments. John Wesley, in his sermon on "The Means of Grace," explains the concept saying: "By means of grace I understand outward signs, words, or actions ordained of God, and appointed to this end—to be the ordinary channels whereby he might convey to men preventing, justifying, or sanctifying grace."[17] The sacraments, for Wesley, are the ways in which God comes to us. In Wesley's account, the outward sign of God's inward grace (gift) reminds us of our call to be responsible and respond outwardly, without which the sacraments are not completed.

In terms of contemporary approaches, several different forms of theological concepts arise regarding the meaning and practice of the sacrament. I will present three representative authors whose work enhances our understanding of sacramental practice. Odo Casel, for example, brings back the concept of mystery. He says, " . . . the fathers teach us the mysteries flow in water and blood from the Lord's side." He also claims that, "mystery means the heart of the action, that is to say, the redeeming work of the risen Lord."[18] It is interesting to think about how Casel relates the concept of mystery to the redemptive acts of Christ made present in sacramental practice. For him, the Church and mystery are inseparable. It is precisely through the liturgy of the Church that the mystery of Christ is carried on and made actual. "Here [in the mystery of worship] Christ performs his saving work, invisible, but present in Spirit and acting upon all men of goodwill,"[19] Casel writes. I think that Casel opens up the possibility of developing the redemptive and transformative character of Christ's mystery, invisible but evident in the sacramental praxis of the Church. The transformative and redemptive acts of Christ emerge in the sacraments. The corporate community transformed by and through Christ's paschal mystery, that is to say, by and through living sacramental liturgy, is called to prophetically proclaim and reclaim Christ's redemptive acts in everyday life inside and outside the church.

David Power incorporates an ethical component into the concept of sacrament. He says that, "the poetics of sacrament in a more recent phase of renewal explores diverse avenues to let the insight into human life, into

16. Ibid., 49.

17. Outler and Heitzenrater, eds., *John Wesley's Sermons*, 160.

18. Casel, "Mystery and Liturgy," 30–31.

19. Ibid., 29.

the being of humans in the world, into the action of God's Word and Spirit, surface in language and rite."[20] Power's understanding makes an important contribution to the renewal of the sacramental praxis grounded in social transformation.

Louis-Marie Chauvet approaches the question of whether we tie the sacrament too closely to life or not from two angles. He is conscious that this is an ambiguous pastoral question. On the one hand, there is the conception of sacramental discourse connected with the whole of a believer's existence. In light of this perspective, Chauvet raises some political questions. For example, he asks: (a) "Does this community have pastoral concern for the welcome of immigrants?" (b) "Is it an active party in promoting reconciliation between rival groups in the community?" (c) What baptism and what Eucharist for which Church?"[21] On the other hand, Chauvet is attentive to the quality of the signs of the sacramental celebration. He asks: (a) "Didn't the desire to tie the sacrament too closely to 'life' run the risk of reducing the mystery?" (b) "Doesn't insisting too strongly that the community be the living sign of what one celebrates, set up a disastrous elitism for the Church and does not that forget that Christ came 'not only for the just, but for the sinners?'"[22] These two critiques reveal a sensibility of a broad understanding of what must be considered when the community intends to live sacramental praxis in its totality with a well balanced consciousness. From this perspective, I can say that there are theological, political, sociological, anthropological, cultural, and economic implications in considering the fullness of the sacramental meaning.

The beauty of sacramental praxis is that it challenges us to think communally. Going against the current of economic systems, in sacramental language one is reminded to put communal necessity before individual preferences. The key toward transformation, renewal, and unity is to engage the community of faith in active ministries—a sign of commitment with and for the created world. One of the most evident commitments of the earlier Christian communities was to be prepared in order to serve the neighbor. It implies a self-offering for the sake of the collectivity as a prompt response to God's call. The study of early sacramental practice reveals an awareness of self-offering to the collective well-being, an engaged prophetic action, as an interconnected action between contemplative spirituality and

20. Power, *Sacrament*, 16.

21. Chauvet, "Rituality and Theology," 195.

22. Ibid.

engaged participation in the world, otherwise known as the "big-house" in which we live.

From the perspective of living a prophetic sacramental life in the world—hearing the past, sincerely reclaiming its memory; analyzing the present, critically proclaiming its redemption; and envisioning the future, intensely anticipating its transformation—what is at stake is the challenge of understanding the meaning of the sacraments as a committed spirituality for the well being of everyone in the world which is created for all, not just for some. This is a capacity rooted in prophetic criticism that has the potential to transform the undesired order. The prophetic understanding of sacrament points toward unity, reconciliation, and transformation. This assumption is rooted in an ethical understanding of the concept of sacrament. The pleasure of worshipping God together and the enjoyment of serving our neighbor are points of departure in prophetic praxis and the sacraments are the reference point and foundation.

By celebrating its sacramental life of the church, the community expresses deeply its vocation to be open to all people who are hungry and thirsty for life in the world. The sacraments represent a significant place to express the prophetic understanding of the community of faith. A celebrating community with a deep sense of its sacramental life must present alternatives to solve any form and structure of oppression and must find liturgical ways to talk about them. In the context of prophetic praxis, the Church must be an open space for change and transformation and the sacraments must constitute the most significant places in which the church reflects such prophetic dimension. Indeed, it is urgent for the Church to be an agency of proclamation and a voice that cries out for liberation from all kinds of oppressive situations in which human beings are crushed to the earth. From the prophetic perspective, we act sacramentally when we acknowledge that sacrament is an extremely powerful experience to change our minds, to transform social-political-economic systems for the sake of the collectivity.

The chief reference for a living sacramental praxis, as an answer to God's call, is to be able to understand God's language (theology) as it functions in all liturgical acts (ritual). Understanding the dimension of this mystery is the beginning of the self-offering in order to serve others in response to God's first commandment. From this perspective it should be inferred that all sacramental praxis, all human relationships, and all environmental consciousness must be rooted in a genuine gesture of love. In this sense, the primary goal of all different kinds of Christian ministry in this "globalized" world is to radiate love, a source of inspiration to all.

Indeed the sacraments are the fullest way a Christian can experience the grace of God for the sake of God's mission in the world. They are genuinely "doing something;" they have significance beyond the ceremony of the ritual itself. It is through the sacraments that Christ greets us, reveals his paschal mystery, assures God's promised blessings, and affirms the eschatological presence of the Holy Spirit, in anticipation of the coming of God's kingdom. In experiencing the sacraments the community of faith is involved in the future hope of the fulfillment of the Kingdom of God, which otherwise could not be accomplished. As Dwight Vogel would say, the sacraments nourish our spiritual body just as food for pilgrims.[23]

The sense of belonging and connection are one of the most expressive characters of the sacramental life. *Oikoumene* dwells in that reality. Sacraments are communal celebrations in the *oikoumene* sense. They embrace all God's children in one *big-house*, the one indivisible body of Jesus Christ, who is the Sacrament *par excellence*.[24] As we will see momentarily, it is through baptism that the community of faith is challenged to act out a social sacred drama, which announces the incorporation into Christ's paschal mystery, a gift for humankind as such.

The next two sections will address the sacramental praxis of the Church as it is perceived through the Baptism and the Eucharist, the ultimate means of transformation. In attempting to make the case that the sacraments have significance beyond the ritual itself and are mediations of socio-political-economic changes, the two sections that follow will offer insights for a dialogue on sacraments as transformative mediation consisting of more than mere signs of water, bread, and wine. They are more than rites and symbolic events. They actually embody and put transformation into action. A number of important questions come to mind as we anticipate the discussion on the sacramental praxis of the church: What concepts or notions does Christianity have for a living sacramental life committed to social, economic, and political issues? Does Christian community express

23. This is not a direct quote from Dwight Vogel, but it is a concept present in his teachings and writings. See, Vogel, *Food for Pilgrims*, 1996.

24. Schillebeeckx says that Christ is the *primordial sacrament* or sacrament of God. According to him, "the man Jesus, as the personal visible realization of the divine grace of redemption, is the sacrament, the primordial sacrament, because this man, the Son of God himself, id intended by the Father to be in his humanity the only way to the actuality of redemption" (see Schillebeeckx, *Christ the Sacrament of the Encounter with God*, 15).

such a foundational reality in which the political and symbolic schemes of language, action, and representation are precisely conceived as a search for identity of the community through sacramental life? What are the implications for the Christian community as it seeks to incorporate in its sacramental praxis the all-important element of prophetic engagement in society?

BAPTISM: LIVING WATER, CHANGING LIFE

One of the chief goals of this book is to show how we can understand and live prophetically the fullness of the sacramental life of the church. Part of this process includes becoming aware of the meaning and relevance of the sacrament for the development of a Christian life engaged in the world seeking eco-socio-economic justice. One of the implications of this goal is to recognize that the Church's sacramental practices in general and baptism in particular, are subjects, which contribute to the shaping of Christian identity.[25] Keeping in mind the following questions will be helpful as we try to understand the importance of the sacramental life for the shaping of Christian identity and the prophetic mission of the church. What does it mean today, to the communities of Christian faith, to talk about a theology of sacramentality? What concepts or notions does Christianity have about its sacramental life? Since grace is the ultimate essence of the sacraments, how does the community of faith conceive the primordial theological concept of grace as distinct from measurable value, like the *manna* in the desert (Exod 16:9–21), where "those who gathered much had nothing over, and those who gathered little had no shortage; they gathered as much as each of them needed (Exod 16:18)?

Even though Christian identity is not restricted to the sacramental life of the Church, the study of the sacrament (as we saw in the first part of this chapter) among all related themes in the liturgical field, is an important and inevitable part of any theological approach to the matter of identity. In Latin America, for example, the advent of the theology of liberation prompted the discussion of identity not only in theological contexts but also political,

25. In his book *Symbol and Sacrament*, Chauvet proposes "a foundational theology of sacramentality" that, in essence, uncovers the marks proper of Christian identity. This is considered especially in the Second Part of his study (chapters 5–8) where he situates the sacraments as part of the structure of Christian identity. See Chauvet, *Symbol and Sacrament*, 161–316.

historical, economic, and social fields. It still remains a significant issue for debates related to those humanistic fields. In Latin America, the theme of identity has been a source of inspiration for writers such as José Míguez Bonino who wrote *Rostros del Protestantismo Latinoamericano*[26] in which he describes the many faces of the Latin American Protestantism with its characteristic diversity: liberal, evangelical, pentecostal, and ethnic. In short, Bonino is addressing, delineating, and claiming the theme of identity for the Latin American Protestant Churches. There is no question about the relevance of Bonino's argument. It has remarkable significance for social and religious studies about Protestant identity in Latin America.

In my view, an accurate conversation about Christian identity has to consider, in conjunction with the more humanistic or secular fields, the sacramentality of the Church—its liturgical life, its religious expressions, and its rituality. Sacramental understanding, however it is conceived, is an incontestable part of Christian identity. According to Aidan Kavanagh, "This is what initiation in the fullest sense disciplines one for: it is the Church."[27] Sacramentality is the Church in its fullest sense. It defines both the Christian and the Church. Kavanagh recalls Victor Turner's concepts of liminality and *communitas* when describing baptism as means of the Church's identity formation. He writes, "Baptism in its fullness is the primary liminal experience during which the Church is shaped each paschal season into a *communitas* of equals in one Body of neither Jew nor Greek, master nor slave, male nor female, and is prepared to receive fresh and new God's grace in Jesus and the Anointed One now become life-giving Spirit."[28] What brings Christians together, then, is faith. Kavanagh goes on to say: "This faith is no mere noetic thing but a way of living together: it is the bond which establishes that reciprocal mutuality of relationships we call communion; it is this communion which constitutes the ecclesial real presence of Jesus Christ in the world by grace and character, faith, hope, and charity."[29] Baptism provides this sense of identity. Its ritual forms and transforms the community. Baptismal ritual gives meaning to the church's existence as Body of Christ, a common ground where everybody has a place and is welcome. To use Anderson's and Foley's words, "rituals not only construct

26. Bonino, *Rostros Del Protestantismo Latinoamericano*. For an English version of this book, see Bonino, *Faces of Latin American Protestantism*.

27. Kavanagh, *The Shape of Baptism*, 145.

28. Ibid., 199–200.

29. Ibid., 145.

reality and make meaning . . . rituals are essential and powerful means for making the world a habitable and hospitable place."[30] Certainly, baptismal ritual confirms this assumption and sacramental initiation is the key.

The way the Church understands, conceives and believes the meaning and concept of its baptismal practices will affect (1) its understanding of God's project through the mystery of Jesus Christ (theology), (2) its unity as a member of the body of Christ (ecclesiology), and (3) its cosmic vision and practice to the world (ethics). All these issues are intrinsically related to the prophetic identity of the Church.

Some questions must be raised in this discussion regarding the understanding of Christian baptism as an important sacramental practice of Christian identity. For example, are there any pedagogical weaknesses, in the process of assimilating or learning about the foundation of the Christian life, in which the celebrating community will be affected in its identity as a community of faith through its baptismal experience? At which level does the discussion on the sacramental celebration of baptism strengthen the community in its relation to God, to others, and to the created order? In what way does the understanding of the sacramental praxis of baptism challenge the Church to assimilate its Christian identity as an agent of prophetic transformation? The purpose of addressing these specific questions is to develop a dialectical way of thinking about this important issue in order to perceive consistently the real meaning of the subject and to foster further prophetic action whose aim is transformation.

The purpose of this section is not to provide an exhaustive survey of the development in the sacramental life of the Christian church, specifically baptism. Nor is it to analyze, assess, or evaluate the theological meaning and the applicability of the concept in its historical trajectory. Rather, the main goal is to spell out the significance of baptism as means of transformation. I will also emphasize the Christian sacramental life of the Church as a serious means to the well being of the whole creation. In short, my main purpose is to awaken the Christian community to understand and to live in the fullness of the sacrament of Baptism, including its meaning and relevance for the development of a Christian life engaged in transforming the world.

In baptism, God has revealed God's self, once and for all, and acted decisively for the renewal of humanity. Through the vicarious nature of Jesus Christ's death and resurrection, the baptized community is reconciled

30. Anderson and Foley, *Mighty Stories, Dangerous Rituals*, 20, 22.

to the wholeness of God, the source of new life for all. New life is the gift of the Spirit given in baptism. This gift of new life is a life of union with Christ and Christ's body, the Church. As a recipient of this gift of divine grace, the baptized community is committed to the ministry of Jesus Christ to the world, making visible new life in prophetic acts. In baptism, the community is given a task of prophetic commitment to participate in Christ's mission of reconciling humanity to God, to one another, and to God's creation. This task implies a life lived in the midst of conflicts and ambiguities while struggling for peace, justice and freedom, as this is how Christ lived. Through baptism the community of faith is shaped and prepared to share the life Christ lived.

My concern is the prophetic nature and ethical character of the response of the baptized community. The idea is not to advocate that such a response represents a condition of baptism. Rather, what I am suggesting is the understanding of baptismal practice in its completeness—a completeness which requires of the baptized ones a response to the unconditional gift (grace) of God in Jesus Christ through the Holy Spirit in effective acts that have more than mere subjective significance. Thus, baptism also involves a prophetic response. It is nothing more than a response to the appropriation of the divine saving action. It implies an active prophetic participation as a commitment to God's project for the world, a commitment to the unity of the Church, and a commitment with the self.

Given the above prophetic reference to the baptismal praxis of the Church and in addition to what has been already presented, there is a pertinent question at this point: What are the biblical and theological references for a prophetic baptismal understanding?

The biblical foundation for this assumption is immensely rich and deserves careful consideration. An exhaustive examination of all biblical passages would require a separate chapter. My purpose, however, is to bring into our conversation a few biblical texts that support a prophetic baptismal understanding. These biblical sources teach us that in baptism we enter in a living relationship with God in Christ through the Holy Spirit. We are incorporated into the Church and into the mystery of Jesus Christ. Paul has this in mind in Rom 6:1–14 where he writes that by baptism we are united in Christ's death and resurrection so we "might walk in newness of life." I understand this "newness of life" as intimate relationship with the wholeness of God that calls for committed relationship with the community of faith, with God's creation, and with the self. It is the visibility of God's grace given in the baptism. By walking in newness of life, we take responsibility to share God's baptismal grace within the baptized community and in the world, as an agent of transformation seeking new life for all.

Through baptism we are made one body (though many different members) united into Christ's body. The apostle Paul says, "As *many* of you as were baptized in to Christ have clothed yourselves with Christ. There is no longer Jew or Greek, there is no longer slave or free, there is no longer male and female; for *all* of you are *one* in Christ Jesus" (Gal 3:27–28). Paul brings this same understanding in his first letter to the Corinthians saying, "For just as the body is *one* and has *many* members, and *all* the members of the body, though *many*, are *one* body, so it is with Christ. For in the *one* Spirit we were *all* baptized into *one* body—Jews or Greek, slaves or free—and we were *all* made to drink of *one* Spirit" (1 Cor 12:12–13).[31] These passages illustrate that in baptism God unites us, with no distinction, into the one body of Christ. We are made a community of equals—children, women, men, rich, and poor. Daniel T. Benedict Jr. maintains that, "in baptism God erases all human distinctions and prideful exclusiveness, joining us as members of the body of Christ."[32] Baptism is a sacrament of inclusivity.

Through baptism the community of faith engages itself in prophetic acts incorporating all people in the one body of Christ as equals; as one body, one Spirit, one hope, one Lord, one faith, one baptism, one God (Eph 4:4–6). This egalitarian dimension of baptism extends in some way to social, economic, and political orders as well. The early community of Acts showed this egalitarian dimension in prophetic acts by sharing their common material wealth "as any had need" (Acts 2:45) until "there was not a needy person among them" (Acts 4:34). This sense of supporting each other enables the community of faith to understand baptism in its fullness. As Robert L. Browning and Roy A. Reed have written, "At its deepest levels baptism is the symbol of our unity as God's family."[33] The sense of belonging to God's family is one of the biblical perspectives that can ensure the prophetic dimension of baptismal practice.

In Luke, when the crowds came to be baptized by John the Baptist asking, "What then should we do?" John the Baptist replied saying, "Whoever has two coats must share with anyone who has none; and whoever has food must do likewise" (Luke 3:11). To the tax collectors, he said, "Collect no

---

31. Emphasis mine.

32. Benedict Jr., *Come to the Waters*, 26.

33. Browning and Reed, *The Sacraments in Religious Education and Liturgy*, 240.

more than the amount prescribed for you" (Luke 3:13). And to the soldiers, John the Baptist said, "Do not extort money from anyone by threats or false accusation, and be satisfied with your wages" (Luke 3:14). From these passages it is clear that the radical social, economic, and political dimensions implied in Christian praxis have a close connection to the baptismal spiritual dimension of repentance and for the forgiveness of sins. As Maxwell E. Johnson affirms, "What John proclaimed, anticipated, and ritually enacted, in typical prophetic fashion, was the dawning of God's decisive intervention in history, the beginning of God's cleansing, restoration, and transformation of God's people."[34] Johnson also notes that "Jesus' submission to John's 'baptism of repentance for the forgiveness of sins' would challenge the early christological claim that Jesus was one who 'knew no sin' (2 Cor 5:21) and was 'without sin' (Heb 4:15)."[35] Herman C. Waetjen presents a convincing argument on the matter of Jesus' being baptized in John's baptism of repentance for the forgiveness of sins. In his exegetical study of Mark's pericope of Jesus' baptism (Mark 1:1–11), Waetjen says, "Surrendering himself to John's baptism, Jesus alone expresses the repentance that God's forerunner was demanding. In effect, he drowned; he died eschatologically; he embraced the reality of his death before his physical expiration . . . It is a genuine act of repentance."[36] Waetjen presents a social, political, and economic approach, affirming that through his baptism Jesus challenges human structures of oppression and of dispossession and inaugurates a new order, the kingdom of God. He continues:

> As such [a genuine act of repentance] it ends Jesus' participation in the structures and values of his society. It concludes his submission to the moral order into which he was born, in which he has been nurtured, and in which he is to realize his potentiality. The entire redemptive process of Jewish society as it is maintained by the institutions through which power is ordered—the temple and its priesthood, the Great Council of the Sanhedrin and its dispensation of justice, the scribes and the Pharisees and their guardianship of the law, the Roman administration and its military forces of occupation, its political oppression and economic exploitation, indeed the totality of the Jewish-Roman social construction of reality—has been terminated by his "death" experience. . . . The death experience of repentance has redeemed Jesus from his

34. Johnson, *The Rites of Christian Initiation*, 10.
35. Ibid., 13.
36. Waetjen, *A Reordering of Power*, 68.

> comprehensive indebtedness and the prescribed ways and means
> of discharging his obligations. As a result, he has become wholly
> unobliged![37]

Waetjen's understanding is that in baptism Jesus rises from the water as the "New human being." My understanding of Jesus' baptism is that it establishes a transformative reality in the world, as well as a new paradigm for prophetic praxis, preparing the way of the Lord. This transformative reality is the establishment of a new order of human relationship, the rupture of unjust political systems, and the redemptive hope for the oppressed and dispossessed.

The theological approach to a prophetic baptismal understanding can be examined by considering a variety of sources. Even though there is no evidence of a systematic study by a particular theologian on the subject of the prophetic dimension of baptism seeking socio-economic justice, this does not preclude having access to a number of sources written by liturgical theologians that have significant bearing on the subject at hand.

Ruth C. Duck suggests that, "to be baptized is to take part in a new constellation of relationships with God, the baptized community, and the world."[38] This metaphor not only helps the church to understand baptism in its completeness, but it can also foster the revitalization of its sacramental praxis as means of transformation. As she also argues, "Through the equality given in baptism, the community is to embody relationships of justice and respect among all people and thus to live out a new reality and provide a foretaste of God's reign in the world."[39] Indeed, this way of thinking about baptism speaks of mutual relationships with God, the community, the world, *and the self*[40] seeking the fullness of human dignity.

Robert L. Browning and Roy A. Reed make an important contribution by affirming baptism as grace. In baptism grace is manifested as the symbols of "new relationship of love and trust with God and others—relationships which, in fact, create an environment of grace, acceptance, forgiveness, and reconciliation."[41] They also believe that: "Baptism is a powerful symbol of the grace of God which was made brilliantly and powerfully visible in Christ and in which the baptized participates joyously, accepting the re-

---

37. Ibid., 68–69.

38. Duck, "Expansive Language in the Baptized Community," 287.

39. Vogel (ed.), *Primary Sources of Liturgical Theology*, 289–290.

40. My Emphasis.

41. Browning and Reed, *The Sacraments in Religious Education and Liturgy*, 242.

sponsibility to continue making visible such grace throughout his or her life in varying ministries within and beyond the body of Christ. Baptism is an ordination of those who are engrafted into the body of Christ. The church is called to continue making visible God's grace, love, and radical justice in the world. The vocation of every member of the body is ministry—the universal priesthood of all believers."[42] This affirmation of individual commitment implies, in a baptismal understanding, going beyond personal isolated commitment. Baptism is far more than a simple private event. It has corporate implications. As a community of faith united in baptism, we are challenged to be relational and inclusive. The relational and inclusive aspects of baptism, as Duck sees it, foster baptismal equality. Duck argues that the equality given through baptism "is based on God's love signed and sealed in baptism."[43] She also calls our attention to the fact that, "The ministry of the baptized community is to love and care for *all* persons and *all* creation, to heal and not to harm, to bring justice, not to condone violence by our words and actions."[44] My sense is that as a community of faith embraced by the fullness of the baptismal meaning, we are called to praxis a ministry prophetically involved in the communal struggle for human rights where they are thwarted by oppressive regimes, unjust economic systems, distrustful political power, and unbalanced ecology on earth.

In his essay, "Three New Initiation Rites," Laurence Stookey surveys and offers insightful comments on the initiation rites of the American Episcopal, United Methodist, and North American Lutheran churches. Even though this is not Stookey's conclusion, I understand his study to support my approach to the prophetic dimension of the sacramental practice of baptism. The most common thread among the three rites is perceived in their common understanding of baptism as covenant. It is from that perspective that Stookey's analysis supports my view. More specifically, he writes:

> The covenant dimension of baptism extends beyond local congregational life. The new liturgies emphasize the conviction that the whole people of God are bound together in service to the total creation. The Lutheran intercessions contain the petition that those about to be baptized may "always and everywhere witness to the Lord by word and life." Both the Episcopal and United Methodist services clearly state the implications of discipleship in social

42. Ibid., 243–244.

43. Duck, "Expansive Language in the Baptized Community," 289.

44. Ibid., 291; emphasis is mine.

terms. In the Episcopal rite candidates are asked: "Will you seek and serve Christ in all persons, loving your neighbor as yourself?" and also, "Will you strive for justice and peace among all people, and respect the dignity of every human being?" The United Methodist service seeks "allegiance to the kingdom which [Christ] has opened to people of all ages, nations, and races;" it then goes on to ask, "Will you resist evil, injustice, and oppression in whatever guises they present themselves?" Finally, the candidate pledges "to serve as Christ's representative in the world."[45]

Stookey's analysis of these three initiation rites reflects my understanding of the meaning of baptism as a means of transformation. If Christian initiation is conceived as a process in which evangelization, welcoming, nurturing, formation, learning, integration, engagement in ministry, mission, and fellowship are all assimilated as patterns of the community's spiritual growth and care, then the baptismal sacrament will take its rightful place in the life and prayer of the church family and will be a sign of transformation.

James L. Empereur also calls our attention to the baptismal rite of the United Methodist Church when he refers to it at the point where the candidate is asked, "Do you renounce the bondage of sin and the injustices of the world?" Empereur concludes, "Those injustices include lifestyles and social structures which give unfair advantage to some over others."[46] The church must not move away from social, political, and economic issues, which directly affect the equality among people and their right to live as dignified human beings who are children of God.

As a baptized community, we must also work towards the transformation of society so that justice, love, peace, and equality may truly permeate every aspect of society. As Don Saliers sees it, "Baptism is the sacrament of radical equality."[47] For Maxwell E. Johnson, baptism "is the 'Great Equalizer.'"[48] My view of this metaphor, creatively suggested by Johnson, helps to illustrate that baptism can be the source which harmonizes all socio-economic distortions, brings together cultural differences, and projects a sound cluster of dignified human beings. Johnson more fully expresses his view saying:

45. Stookey, "Three New Initiation Rites," 283.

46. Empereur and Kiesling, *The Liturgy That Does Justice*, 49.

47. Saliers, *Worship and Spirituality*, 55. White, referring to the same idea about baptism says: "It is the sacrament of equality." See White, *Sacraments as God's Self Giving*, 96.

48. Johnson, *The Rites of Christian Initiation*, 366.

It [baptism—the "Great Equalizer"] transcends all such distinctions and, as such, provides us with a perspective and foundational basis from which we might address any and all forms of racism, classism, and sexism. For here in baptism—as on the day of Pentecost itself (one of the great New Testament paradigms for Christian baptism)—are the divisions of the Tower of Babel reversed and all again become initiated into Christ as one people, speaking a common language of prayer, thanksgiving, and witness. Here in baptism is the paradise of Genesis 1 and 2 restored where God is most appropriately imaged by the unity of both male and female. Here rich and poor come together as equals, clothed in the baptismal garments of Christ, and take their place together at the banquet table.[49]

In baptism, the community of faith finds its own journey toward a new spirituality. This baptismal spirituality, which must be experienced daily as Martin Luther suggests,[50] announces the community's commitment to new life for all. Saliers rightly contends that, "Baptism sets up a wide range of explicit and implicit possibilities for human existence."[51] What the community needs to embrace is not only the explicit theological concepts of the sacramental practice of baptism. It should also embrace baptism's implicit prophetic implications for the life of the world. This understanding has a dialectical prophetic connotation that challenges our baptismal spirituality. Saliers emphasizes this dialectical approach in his discussion on baptism declaring: "Sins are forgiven—so how shall we live with one another? We are incorporated into Christ's body on earth—so how can we show that we belong to him? We have union with Jesus' work—so how can we be Christ for a broken and starving and death-bent world? We have received the gift of the Holy Spirit—so how shall those gifts for ministry and all fruits of the Spirit be manifest in our lives? We have been born anew—so how shall we

---

49. Ibid.

50. Luther's statement is frequently employed, but none of the resources used here shows Luther's direct source. The quotation is as follows: "Every time you wash your face you should remember that you have been baptized." Stookey presents a similar quote from Luther emphasizing the daily baptismal spirituality, but without the reference of washing the face. As many other scholars do, Stookey does not present Luther's direct source. Stookey says, "Luther sought to emphasize the daily renewal of the baptismal covenant by suggesting to his followers that, each morning upon arising, they place a hand upon the head (where the water of the sacrament had been applied) and say, 'I am baptized'" (see Stookey, *Baptism*, 75).

51. Saliers, *Worship and Spirituality*, 50.

grow toward maturity and into the full stature of the humanity of Christ?"[52] The questions posed by Saliers challenge our daily communal spirituality. It must be emphasized that these questions are addressed to "we," not to the individual "I." It does support the baptismal understanding as a process in which all people in the congregation must be engaged and renewed in a living baptismal consciousness.

To those thoroughly committed to participate in Jesus' ministry, it is possible to add immeasurable challenges towards the celebration of an engaging prophetic baptismal spirituality. It must be remembered daily (in Luther's sense) and celebrated intensively by the whole congregation whenever baptism is performed, in connection to the church's unlimited creative liturgical life. A prophetic baptismal spirituality integrates the whole community to share its commitment and covenant to the Triune God, in love to one another, to the neighbor, to the rich or poor, and to the whole creation. This spiritual posture requires the church to review its baptismal understanding. This new lens will direct the church to the inevitable re-examination of its Christian education system, the point of measurement of the community's good spiritual health. The Christian education system of the church will tremendously affect its sacramental understanding and living. Regarding the baptismal understanding, Saliers writes: "When our baptismal understandings are weak, our understanding of the nature and character of the entire Christian life is weak."[53] A living baptism points to a continuous formation process. This will be a cyclic process in which Christian faith will never cease to grow. The community of the baptized, transformed by the power of the Holy Spirit through water and formed by the baptismal paradigm, will be a living source pouring life, love, and praise where everyone will be gathered, nurtured, and sent to fulfill God's will into the created order.

EUCHARIST: SACRAMENTAL EXCHANGES FOR THE LIFE OF THE WORLD

Christian engagement in social, economic, and political issues challenge our Christian sacramental understanding. Engagement must be understood as social-political active participation. It is impossible to be engaged in any kind of social-political movement without an external form of

52. Ibid.

53 Ibid., 45.

consciousness manifested in concrete acts of participation; not pseudo-participation, but committed involvement; not with an alienating way of thinking, but with critical consciousness.[54] Eucharistic celebration challenges our political consciousness. In celebrating the Eucharist, Christians remember the offering and sacrifice of Jesus Christ, God's gift for the life of the world. Celebrating the Eucharist with a political consciousness requires the understanding that it is a communal exchange act in which one receives the gift and returns it to others. If one celebrates Jesus' Table alone or for self-benefit, there is no exchange whatsoever. It is true that an exchanging process happens in communal context or in personal spiritual relationship with God—one receives God's gift and returns thanksgiving. The challenge, from a prophetic perspective, is to share, with thanksgiving, the gift received as source of life, peace and justice for the world.

In Jesus' Feast, the community performs a communal remembrance of his offering for others. Because Christ's body was given to us, we are challenged to give our lives as gifts for the nourishment of others. This committed gesture is as political as Christ's was. The political connotation of this gesture focuses on Christ's request to "Do this in remembrance of me" not as a romantic remembrance, but as a resisting and denouncing remembrance in accord with Christ's ministry against the established means of power and oppression of his time. In addition, Christ's Eucharistic body needs to be remembered in this political way. The gesture of taking, breaking, blessing, and giving the bread has in its foundation the imperative political claim to resist hunger, oppression, violence, and unjust socio-economic order. What we need to remember is Christ's way of living, which has in its essence the prophetic action proclaiming the Kingdom of God, the good news of human liberation.

William Cavanaugh, in his book *Torture and Eucharist*, opens up foundational questions related to Christian ecclesiology, theology of the political, and sacramental theology.[55] As mentioned previously, engagement implies an active social participation with critical consciousness. Paulo Freire reminds us that this will result in "not a pseudo-participation,

---

54. Critical consciousness is one of Freire's imperatives for effective participation in society. Committed involvement and critical consciousness suggest a political predisposition for the benefit of others. See Freire, *Education for Critical Consciousness*. Also see Freire, *Pedagogy of the Oppressed*.

55. Cavanaugh, *Torture and Eucharist*.

but committed involvement."[56] Committed involvement and critical consciousness suggest a political predisposition for the benefit of others.

Cavanaugh's determination to ponder the Christian social-political life and praxis corroborate this assertion. In considering this reality, Cavanaugh argues that "religion is not necessarily privatized, hidden from the public view, but the church takes its rightful place in civil society, and occupies itself directly with the social."[57] He also says, "the church is not a separate sanctuary, but is part and parcel of the politics and economics of the world."[58] In this sense, the church is the ecclesiological body of Christ inserted in the society. The church is the *ekklesia*, God's people together, *koinonia*, communion at full stretch. Communion here reflects the church, the Eucharist, and the ultimate communion: the world—the great inhabited house.

Cavanaugh also suggests a significant political perspective for a sacramental understanding: Eucharistic ecclesiology. From this perspective, the celebrating community is structured upon the performance of the Eucharist, embodying a "counter-politics" to the politics of the world. In this sense, the Eucharist resists all kinds of politics and violent disciplines of the world that violate human dignity. Cavanaugh argues that the Christian practice of the political is embodied in the Eucharist. In considering this reality, he argues further that the church is the ecclesiological body of Christ inserted in society. Here, the church is seen as part of the politics and economics of the world. From this perspective, the Eucharist is truly social and political. It affects the community's "social imagination."[59]

In reality, the arguments presented above are evidence of a social fragility that reflects deeply in our understanding of the church as the Body of Christ who suffered and still suffers through human and institutional actions against the individual and collective social body. The violence against a human body is also violence against Christ. The issue here is not just to denounce signs of violence; it also points out the unjust political and economic systems that, hidden through the image of "development," dignify signs of anti-life throughout the world. Social, political, and economic

56. Freire, *Pedagogy of the Oppressed*, 51.

57. Cavanaugh, *Torture and Eucharist*, 4.

58. Ibid., 13.

59. Ibid., 12. "Social imagination" is the expression Cavanaugh uses to designate the social "vision which organizes the members into a set of coherent performances, and which is constantly reconstructed by those performances." It does not imply an "unreal fantasy."

injustices are an ecclesiological problem and must be addressed. Prophetic Eucharistic celebration is definitely the theological ground to proclaim unconditional life for the created world and all human beings.

The issue at stake here is the political understanding that individual integrity is directly related to social dignity. They are not separate from each other. One of Cavanaugh's aims is to "display a kind of Eucharistic counter-politics which forms the church into a body capable of resisting oppression."[60] The theological ground for this assertion is the Eucharistic celebration itself. It expresses the ultimate level of individual integrity for the sake of social dignity.

Violence against Christ's body is also part of this political-theological understanding. Jesus was tortured to death. It is also Cavanaugh's argument that "the Eucharist is the church's response to torture, and the hope for Christian resistance to the violent disciplines of the world."[61] In torture, as more clearly evidenced in Christ's torture, power over the body is a manifested violence not only against the individual bodies but against social bodies as well.

It is at Jesus' Table where a Christian praxis of the political is embodied. Jesus' paschal mystery, life, passion, death, resurrection, ascension, sending of the Spirit and promise of the Second Coming, is the proclamation of God's political redemptive project assuming the church, its potential, as the "true body of Christ" (*corpus verum*). This is the basis for the church's social praxis supported by its Eucharistic celebration. To unfold the whole significance of the sacramental system of the Christian Church, its theological formalization, its liturgical expression, its ethical relevance, and its political ideological body function, we must discern its multiple languages in which the complex system of Christian identity has its roots: Christ's paschal mystery. Prophetic Eucharistic celebration embodies this assertion and proclaims both the invisible (*corpus mysticum*) and visible (*corpus verum*)[62] body of Christ—sacramental and ecclesiological, as they

---

60. Ibid., 14.

61. Ibid., 2.

62. The above assumption, presented in Cavanaugh's argument on the distinction between the sacramental and ecclesial body of Christ, *corpus mysticum* and *corpus verum*, is also carefully developed by Pickstock, but from a different perspective even though she uses Henri de Lubac's study as Cavanaugh does. She approaches the matter from the late medieval theological opposition between "mystical" and "real" that is inscribed to the eucharistic body itself. The political element inferred from Pickstock's argument is that the gradual understanding toward the juxtaposition of the "mystical" and "real,"

relate to each other proclaiming Christ's paschal mystery: absolute life for the whole of human existence.

I will return to the above subjects momentarily. What does it mean today, to the communities of Christian faith, to connect such a foundational theology of sacramentality to the violence against social bodies? This question is inevitable when it is remembered that the basic idea of the subject of this book derive from concepts related to the social, anthropological, political, economic, and psychological science as developed by classical and contemporary scholars. It reflects how complex, extensive, and endlessly woven is the concept of the sacramentality of the church. We must deal with and assimilate the language of social body. Cavanaugh argues that, "'body' is a crucial metaphor for political and social analysis, and most important the body of Christ is central to Christian theology of the Eucharist and the church."[63] To practice and celebrate the sacraments is to believe in their institution as mediation into the body of Christ, the Church. This is the condition for Christian existence. It links us as members of an institutional body, the Body of Christ. Chauvet once said, "It is thus impossible to conceive of the faith outside of the body."[64] He continues, saying, "there is no faith unless somewhere inscribed, inscribed in a body—a body from a specific culture, a body with a concrete history, a body of desire."[65] Christian communities must recognize the emergent necessity of apprehending the language of the body and its symbolic systems.

The language of the community body must be perceived. The sacraments, especially the Eucharist, have no place to be without the corporeality of the Christian community. This is why Chauvet argues, "One becomes a Christian only by entering an institution and in letting this institution stamp its 'trademark,' its 'character,' on one's body."[66] We can see that Cavanaugh is not alone in this political theological venture. Moreover, what are the implications for celebrating the Eucharist with prophetic commitments? What issues must be raised that substantiate the prophetic dimension of the Eucharistic praxis? In *The Eucharist and the Hunger of the World*,

---

both on the sacramental body and on the body of Christ as church, corroborated by the centralization of clerical administration and the professionalization of the theology that provided the authority to the priest to operate the visible and legible manipulation of the sacramental. See Pickstock, *After Writing*, 158–61.

63. Cavanaugh, *Torture and Eucharist*, 17.

64. Chauvet, *Symbol and Sacrament*, 150.

65. Ibid., 154.

66. Ibid., 155.

Monika Hellwig offers relevant insights for a prophetic commitment through Eucharistic practice. From Hellwig's book, we can extrapolate a paradigm through which the Christian community can build its political praxis supported by a Eucharistic praxis that changes the participants from mere spectators into intimate and committed participants.

The first element in Hellwig's Eucharistic matrix is that the "Eucharist is a sharing of food, not only eating but sharing."[67] The undeniable reality is that the Eucharist is a shared meal, a banquet, a feast, a communal solidarity. As such it provides the most basic necessary provision for life and its nourishment.

"The Eucharist as communion of the faithful" is the concept used by the World Council of Churches' *Baptism, Eucharist, and Ministry* (BEM).[68] Everyone is invited to participate and share in the feast. No one in the community is the owner of the table. The table does not belong to the community. It is God's self-giving love to the whole community. Christ's sacramental presence invites the community to celebrate and share. It is not our table. It is Jesus' Table. This could be stated as one of the theological reasons for the sharing of the feast, as the community of faith celebrates the sacramental gift. BEM also states, "It is in the Eucharist that the community of God's people is fully manifested. Eucharistic celebrations always have to do with the whole Church, and the whole Church is involved in each local Eucharistic celebration."[69] John Wesley, in his sermon "The Means of Grace," argues: "Let all, therefore, who truly desire the grace of God, eat of that bread and drink of that cup."[70] Thus, the political nature of the Eucharist flows out of the eating and sharing the bread in a common-round table where the invitation is for those who truly desire to share and participate in God's grace for all.

Gustavo Gutiérrez, in speaking about the preferential option for the poor, teaches us to know not only how to listen or how to see the reality of poverty, but also how to share. He says: "To break the bread is to share what one has. Jesus gave to them the bread of the word and also gave them the actual bread, the bread that calms hunger, because for Jesus daily life is important. The testaments are clear: the focus is on sharing, not

---

67. Hellwig, *The Eucharist and the Hunger of the World*, 2.

68. *Baptism, Eucharist and Ministry*, 14.

69. Ibid.

70. Outler and Heitzenrater, eds., *John Wesley's Sermons*, 165.

multiplying."[71] The lesson is that we share what we have, not because of abundance or because there is something left. According to Acts 3:6, Peter said: "I have no silver or gold, but what I have I give you." Sharing is the principle of solidarity. According to Hellwig the atmosphere surrounding the Eucharistic meal connects the true body of Christ with human hunger. This connection is undoubtedly political, precisely because it points to the needs of all human beings and challenges political platforms.

The second element in Hellwig's matrix is that in celebrating the Eucharist we experience God's hospitality. In this regard she writes: Every Eucharist we celebrate demands that we ask ourselves individually and collectively where we stand in relation to God's hospitality in the world— whether we are acting as fellow hosts of God's hospitality in the world or trying to corner a monopoly on it.[72] God, through the redemptive character of Christ's incarnation, is the One who welcomes the people to Jesus' hospitable Table.

Metaphorical language such as "hand in hand," "in circle," and "new hands for holding on," to mention just a few, are helpful expressions to declare the unity of the body where acceptance, gathering, friendship, caresses, affection, hugging, love, justice, and peace are strong signs of Christ's presence linking people to one another. Inclusive language is better expressed when it represents the metaphorical way of expressing the profound desire of being ready and able to lift up our hearts while participating and celebrating the Eucharist, whatever our physical condition, socio-economic status, ethnicity, or cultural background. Thus, when the body and blood of Christ are shared, all kinds of intolerance, rejection, racism, sexism separation, socio-economic injustice, disabilities, and lack of liberty are radically challenged. Reconciled and united by the celebration of the Eucharistic gift, the body of Christ is called to be a prophetic agent of reconciliation among human beings and among the created world. The Eucharist is the place where the community's inclusive posture can be expressed as a whole. In that sense, the celebration of the Eucharist as sacramental gift is an invitation to live community in its totality (*koinonia*) and its unity. It is the sacrament of the "common-unity."

God's hospitability is already expressed in creation, the ultimate *koinonia*, where no public and political powers can subvert God's liberating intervention as unconditional gift. In creation there are no questions

71 Gutiérrez, "Renewing the Option for the Poor," 80.

72. Hellwig, *The Eucharist and the Hunger of the World*, 20.

regarding permission to get in, no political subordinations in which to participate, no value exchanges to perpetuate domination. God's hospitability expressed in creation is the theological foundation for a political understanding of a hospitable Table.

The third element in Hellwig's Eucharistic matrix is the mission character of the Eucharistic celebration. Through liturgy, especially through Eucharistic practice, the community of faith proclaims God's redemptive act and announces the genuine compassion for the needy, for the hungry, the destitute, the dispossessed, the lonely, and the marginalized. Hellwig maintains that, from the meaning of the Eucharist, we learn to do Christian mission. She elaborates the point. "What we learn from the Eucharist when we reflect on its meaning in the context of scripture and tradition and in the light of our own human experience is that the Christian mission to the hungry is to enter into their need and find ways to satisfy their hunger, to challenge the structures of the world that keep some peoples and some populations hungry, to question the sick and inordinate desires that maintain those structures."[73]

This idea for Christian mission has its foundation in the totality of Jesus' missionary praxis in offering himself, the true bread of life, challenging the political structures of the world that affirm and sustain signs of death. The political challenge that the Christian church faces in celebrating the sacramental meal is practicing its mission of separating it from its religious dimensions *of* life, which is very different from the conception of the religious dimensions *to* life.

Jesus' Table calls for the fulfillment of mission. This is another characteristic of prophetic Eucharistic celebration. It must send all of us toward the fulfillment of a mission in the world. Word alone, and Table by itself, fails in the totality of their meaning when mission is not fulfilled. When the proclamation of the Word (Gift) becomes united with the gifts of the bread and the cup (Reception), the celebration becomes the sacramental sign of transformation (Return-gift)—a concrete and authentic "liturgy of the neighbor."[74] The community will be prepared to hear Jesus' calling for mission, inviting and challenging it to serve the created world and all human beings as committed agents in proclamation of God's kingdom, which is a sacramental gift. In other words, to celebrate the Eucharist in its totality

73. Ibid., 79.

74. Chauvet, *Symbol and Sacrament*, 265. Chauvet's concept of Gift—Reception—Return—gift will be explored further in chapter 4.

and intensively, we must translate our worship into discipleship, that is, into mission. If Jesus' Table is understood as a gift from God, there is no reason to break the circle, to negate God's gift of grace, which sustains the community as a whole. There is no mission and no prophetic dimension in celebrating the Eucharist when the Word is not understood, when the symbols have no meaning, when the community is not united and linked together, and when the community is not challenged to testify to God's kingdom before the whole creation.

The sacrament of the Table is, in its essence, a communal celebration. Nobody celebrates alone. Around the Table there is no place for loneliness. Our commitment, as a prophetic community, is to share faithfully and joyfully the gifts of God with all human beings.

As Christians committed to life in its totality, we need to assimilate the conviction that the sacramental meal does have social, political, and economic relevance for society at large. As the true body of Christ, we have the mission to extend the true bread of life to humankind.

The last element in this Eucharistic matrix is the celebration of the Eucharist as an opportunity to express our commitment to peace. Hellwig expands the point in a helpful way. "The Eucharist signifies in its multiple symbolism that the way of Christ is peace, and that peace is possible not only in our hearts but in our world with all its ambiguities and all its complexity. Christ has given us a new share in God's hospitality in the Eucharist which is blessing, sacrament and transformation."[75] Because the Eucharist is the celebration of *shalom*, sharing of the peace is an inevitable gesture that addresses every form and structure of anti-peace, confronting them with the image of the Triune God. I see this as a social, political, religious, and cultural community of peace.

There will not be peace in the world if the international community does not hear the history and voices of those who suffer social, economic, cultural, and political oppression by the established empire systems. In a postmodern perspective one needs to deconstruct and subvert the established empire systems, while invoking the hermeneutics of suspicion in the face of claims to universal truth. Such a stance should aid in overcoming suffering, oppression, injustice, and violations against human dignity. The emphasis now is not on an alienating theological and introverted praxis, but on a theologically extroverted, reflective, and engaged praxis. From this perspective, the body of Christ must be shared in a concrete and historical

75. Ibid., 85.

place revealing God's liberating project for humankind. It means that theo-logical praxis has its *sitz im leben* in the concreteness of political con-sciousness. From the perspective of Freire's social-political consciousness learning process, the people once called illiterate by society now participate in the Eucharistic meal as agents of theological knowledge—their own op-pressed lives. Prophetic hope is the point of emphasis. It is the desire to face the impossibilities and to know the transcendent, guided by heart and inner eyes. Through this lens, we can infer that the Eucharist is the place with the most potential for the affirmation of this prophetic hope where the Christian community shares the bread and the wine with God's children and sees reality through Christ's life, death, and resurrection, which is the ultimate *shalom*.

To reveal the whole significance of the prophetic Eucharistic praxis, its theological formalization, its liturgical expression, its ethical relevance, and its politic-ideological function, we must discern the multiple languages in which the complex system of Christian identity has its roots: Christ's paschal mystery. This is a good segue to the discussion in chapter three which focuses more intensively on liturgy as transformation.

3

Liturgy as Means of Transformation

IN THE CLOISTER WALK, Kathleen Norris writes about the "immersion into a liturgical world"[1] which results from daily religious praxis. This is a time for prayers, gestures, songs, antiphons, scripture readings, as well as work, study, play, and service to others. In my view, this liturgical world is a well that overflows in transformation, which challenges Christians to be prepared to serve their neighbors. This transformation involves a self-offering for the sake of the collective whole as a prompt response to God's call. It reflects the assumption that self-offering to the collective well-being is a result of an engaged prophetic action, an interconnected relationship between contemplative spirituality and effective participation in the world. This immersion provides an opportunity to experience both the "Wholly Other," the *mysterium tremendum*,[2] through intimate relationship with the wholeness of the divine, and the "wholly other," as well as with ourselves, with the neighbor, through gestures of love that are characterized by justice, freedom, and peace. It also gives rise to a prophetic response to the circumstances of daily life. In that response, liturgical acts (readings, prayers, songs, tastes, touches, smells and all other expressions of liturgical action) are not ends unto themselves, but acts, which gain meaning when they become signs of life and gestures of love. This immersion into a liturgical world drives worshippers to rediscover religion as a sign of a daily

1. Norris, *The Cloister Walk*, xix.

2. For a reference on the phenomenological concept of God, see Otto, *The Idea of the Holy*, 12–24.

personal and communal encounter with God and with their neighbor. It is a praxis that has its foundations in both *leitourgia* and *diakonia*; in essence, it is a merger between *leitourgia* and *diakonia* in divine-human dialectical relationship, the result of which is a rendering of service unto God and humankind.

As Don Saliers reminds us, "there is a unity of *leitourgia* and *diakonia*—of worship and the doing of good works—implied by the narrative recital of God's covenant and history with the world."[3] Saliers also suggests that the work of the people, worship to God, finds unity in praise and mercy. He writes that, "the tensive unity of *leitourgia* and *diakonia* cannot be reduced. Worship of God is both in the assembly of praise and in the works of mercy."[4] Saliers also asks, "What agencies within liturgy as cultus (leitourgia) prompt and give evidence of the people's liturgy in the world (diakonia)?"[5]

A primary component in this living spirituality, as an answer to God's call and to the *pathos* of human beings, is "You shall love God with all your heart, and with all your soul, and with all your strength, and with all your mind; and your neighbor as yourself." (Luke 10:27) This is the great commandment, the first call for all, and the gift that will remain forever. As a means of transformation, Christian liturgy, then, must be rooted simultaneously in the self-offering gesture of love of the Triune God, and in our commitment to love our neighbor. Understanding the role of love in the mystery of the Trinity is basic to this self-offering to which we are called in order to serve others as a response to God's first commandment.

One of the attributes that describes the Church is that it is a social body, a community. That is, the Church is a community of persons living in communion, *koinonia*, serving God and one another, where everyone is welcome, especially those marginalized by society. The theological foundation for this idea comes from the concept of God as Triune community.[6] Living community is what the Trinitarian God teaches us. In the process of developing our Christian life, we come to realize the Triune God is a living community that is neither distant nor isolated from our own community. God's very presence among us, through us, and in us intensifies even more

---

3. Saliers, "Liturgy and Ethics: Some New Beginnings," 34.

4. Saliers, *Worship as Theology*, 189.

5. Ibid., 180.

6. The theological concept of God as Triune community will be developed in the next section having Boff, LaCugna, and Moltmann as primary esources.

our sense of community. It gives us a transcendental meaning of intimacy. Trinity expresses not three separate persons but communal intimacy, which manifests its deep reality when God becomes flesh with our flesh and spirit with our spirit. I believe that as members of a divine community, living intimately with God and with one another, we, the body of Christ, are called to communicate that truth prophetically, which in the final ultimate analysis is what is known as solidarity. Intimacy and solidarity are siblings born from divine relationship. In the level of supra commitment to one another, the community of faith honors one another's dignity as an image of the Triune God. Such honoring requires that there be no division by race, gender, age, social, cultural, economic, political, or religious differences. *Koinonia* happens through *leitourgia* (the work of the people), where the community embodies the prophetic potential to transform oppressive realities into genuinely inclusive relationships that welcome everyone.

In this chapter, I examine three basic resources for conceiving of liturgy as a means of transformation. The first resource comes from a hermeneutic exercise on the prophetic image of God as a Trinitarian paradigm for transformation. The second resource is based on the understanding that a community of faith needs to build its transformative project based on social, religious, and cultural parameters while assuming its responsibility for social justice, religious commitment, and cultural receptivity. That is to say, to seek transformation a community of faith is called to reflect on its relationship to the world, on the language of its liturgical life, and on its immersion into diverse cultural contexts. The third resource addresses the transformative potential of liturgy, which seeks socio-economic justice. An ongoing dialogue between liturgy and the social sciences contributes to engaging the community as agents of transformation. Two questions can help clarify the claims that this section addresses: How does prophetic liturgy serve as a catalyst in the socio-economic transformation of unjust systems? Does liturgy have anything to do with socio-economic justice? These basic questions address the belief that socio-economic issues can be objects of liturgical praxis and theological reflection, as well as mediation for a transforming and engaging Christian community committed to the well-being of the created order and all people.

THE PROPHETIC IMAGE OF GOD: A TRINITARIAN REFERENCE FOR THE PROPHETIC COMMUNITY'S VOCATION

Let us turn our attention to a Trinitarian prayer I wrote as a theological exercise seeking to find words for worship. The images of the Triune God presented in this prayer are signs of wondering, metaphors of critical consciousness, and cries for transformation. Here, as a reference and source of inspiration for our conversation around the suggested theme, I propose an unusual image of God as prophet, that is, God, as Prophet of prophets; Jesus Christ, as Incarnated Prophet; and the Holy Spirit, as spirit of prophets.

The prayer presented below is meant to unfold meaning and possibilities for the worshipper in such a way that in and through it, she or he finds transformative potential for prophetic praxis. Ruth C. Duck and Patricia Wilson-Kastner, in their co-authored book *Praising God: The Trinity in Christian Worship*, contribute to a study of Trinitarian theology founded on the possibility of a living Trinitarian Christian spirituality. They envision spirituality committed to inclusiveness (gender-inclusive), and to the centrality of the Trinity in Christian faith, worship, and service. They seek "to suggest ways of faithful witness to the triune God, in a constellation of metaphors that includes yet goes beyond the language of 'Father' and 'Son.' In doing so, [they] hope to encourage Trinitarian faith, worship, and life and their expressions in just and loving human relationships."[7] Inclusiveness is a concept that helps us understand and incorporate in our daily language the theological principle of the wholeness of God.

As Christians, we are called to cross the boundaries that separate us from each other and from intimate communion with the divine Trinity. Together we are called to stand hand-in-hand, walking in the cloister of each other's life, knowing each other, sharing our journey, and seeking that day when we all come together in a big round table.

The prophetic Trinitarian model of society, as we will see, emerges from the possibility of seeing, reclaiming, and denouncing: to see what is hidden, to reclaim abundant life, and to denounce oppression. Here, then, is the prayer for our consideration:

> O God, Prophet of prophets,
> light of the world,
> who sees the visible and the invisible:

---

7. Duck and Wilson-Kastner, *Praising God: The Trinity in Christian Worship*, 7.

Come, open our inner eyes to see what
is hidden before us!

O Jesus Christ, incarnate prophet,
light of the world,
who taught us to see beyond all possibilities:
Come, give us courage to reclaim abundant
life for all people!

O Holy Spirit, spirit of prophets,
light of the world,
who illuminates our paths in the midst of all troubles:
Come, help us to denounce the signs of oppression
around the earth!

By reading and praying this prayer, and recognizing its prophetic significance, the community of faith can be challenged to worship the triune God and act prophetically in the world, transforming its *pathos* into the *ethos* of the triune community. As Christians we are called to recognize that we cannot live a prophetic Christian life in this world without a clear awareness of human suffering (human *pathos*); nor can we be prophetic without any sense of injustice and *pathos* of the world, or of God's *ethos*, God's project of self-giving (divine *ethos*) for humanity through the *Incarnated Prophet*, Jesus Christ. With an awakened sensitivity for wonder at the created order, and a reverence for what sustains its stability, and for human dignity, our action will be a sign of transformation and commitment to the well-being of all, not just of some. The celebrating prophetic community, in all its action in the world, must see and contemplate, feel and share, hear and proclaim the "foretaste of glory divine"[8] for all, as Saliers would say.

What are the theological resources for a Trinitarian approach to a prophetic community of faith? Leonardo Boff, Catherine LaCugna, and Jürgen

---

8. "Foretaste of Glory divine" is a phrase from Fanny Crosby's hymn "Blessed Assurance." Saliers uses it in connection with his understanding of Christian liturgy as eschatological art of prayer and action. The last paragraph of his book *Worship as Theology*, states, "In the eschatological art faithfully celebrated, in every time and place and culture, human ears hear things that speak what no ear has yet heard, human eyes see things that manifest that which no eye has yet seen. But such seeing and hearing is faithful when what is prayed becomes a way of justice and mercy. The foretaste of glory divine nurtures the fruits of the Spirit in human history. God's promises hold the future, calling us to taste and see, to work and pray" (see Saliers, *Worship as Theology*, 230). I am also drawing on Saliers's pathos/ethos language.

Moltmann will be of help here because of their contributions to understanding the social character of the relational Triune God.

Leonardo Boff

Leonardo Boff suggests the triune community as a model for any just, egalitarian social organization. He says, "In the beginning is communion."[9] The Trinity, in its social relationship, provides a model of social living. The Triune God, a community of self-giving, announces the paradigm for human communities of self-giving. Through the intimate and transparent level of the relationship of the Trinity, human beings learn the ultimate level of a unity that respects differences. As was suggested by Boff, we can look to an understanding of the triune community to improve society. In Boff, we are challenged to consider the possibility of the communion of the Trinity and its close relation to communion in society, which produces a critical attitude for human understanding of interpersonal relationships. This critical attitude increases the community's awareness of "personhood, community, society, and the church."[10] According to Boff, "The community of the Father, Son and Holy Spirit becomes the prototype of the human community dreamed of by those who wish to improve society and build it in such a way as to make it into the image and likeness of the Trinity."[11] This understanding of Trinitarian relationship leads us to envision prophetically a society structured by unity in diversity, where human relationship is perpetuated by inclusion rather than exclusion, reciprocity rather than exploitation, love rather than abuse, peace rather than violence. What the Trinitarian community shows us is the clear possibility of prophetic resistance against all signs of anti-life.

Jürgen Moltmann

Jürgen Moltmann also gives important insights for discussion on the correlation between the doctrine of the Trinity and human community. He points to the mutual Trinitarian relationship as providing a foundational matrix for the Christian understanding of society, of community.

9. Boff, *Holy Trinity, Perfect Community*, 3.
10. Boff, *Trinity and Society*, 148.
11. Ibid., 7.

For Moltmann, the triune God is a unique community, an eternal divine community. He presents three basic concepts of the Trinity that help to elucidate the understanding of human community. They are: "(1) person, (2) relation, (3) community (*perichoresis*)."[12] These concepts are intimately related to anthropological relationship in society. First, according to Moltmann, the concept of person[13] contains in itself "the concept of unitedness or at-oneness, just as, conversely, the concept of God's at-oneness must in itself contain the concept of the three Persons."[14] Second, the three divine persons are in relationship to one another, with one another, and for one another. As Moltmann sees the Triune relationship, "they are just as much united with one another and in one another."[15] Thirdly, the communal aspect is directly related to a *perichoretic* unity. The Triune community "must be perceived in the perichoresis of the divine Persons."[16] For Moltmann, the anthropological concept of person "has led to an understanding of the human personality with unalienable human rights and has overcome anthropological modalism, which dissolves the person into his or her social functions."[17] Moltmann's insight regarding the correlation between Trinity and human community has led me to understand this basic principle in the context of *communality* and *relationality*, a relationship of mutual affirmation. In Moltmann's account, the three divine persons represent the ultimate level of social relationship, since "they are persons in social relationship."[18] He sees divine relationship as "eternal perichoresis," the ultimate level of

12. Moltmann-Wendel and Moltmann, *Humanity in God*, 96. For Boff, the three key foundational concepts for theological reflection on the Trinity are: "the concept of life, communion, and perichoresis." See Boff, *Trinity and Society*, 124.

13. For the sake of convenience, I continue to use the term "person" to designate each "entity" of the Trinity. However, I am mindful that this is only one way of referring to the elements within the Trinity. Ramshaw points to other theological expressions to describe the Triune God: fourth-century Greek theologians—"one divine essence in three *hypostases*"; Augustine—"If we say three persons, it is not so much to affirm something as to avoid saying nothing"; Karl Barth—"modes of being"; Karl Rahner—"ways of being"; and finally, referring to Catherine LaCugna, Ramshaw says that "some theologians hope that appropriate use of *the divine person* can help define *the human person* better." Even though Ramshaw does not present a suggestion, she seems to agree that the use of the term "person" is not the most appropriate. See Ramshaw, *God Beyond Gender*, 82–83.

14. Moltmann, *The Trinity and the Kingdom*, 150.

15. Ibid.

16. Ibid.

17. Moltmann-Wendel and Moltmann, *Humanity in God*, 97.

18. Ibid.

unity and mutual relationship. For me, this points to the ultimate level of prophetic action towards equality, resistance against oppressed subordination, and intolerance to race, gender, class, and other distinctiveness that separate and alienate persons from each other and from God.

One of Moltmann's remarkable contributions is his short but insightful essay, "The Triune God: Rich in Relationships." Here he says that the Church, as an "icon of the Trinity," has been a community of freedom and equality, which "illuminates the image of the triune God." He continues:

> This is best expressed in the base communities in Latin America and in some Pentecostal communities, communities of social justice and personal freedom, modeled on the communities of the early church which lacked nothing because they held all in common . . . we can move beyond the human community and into the creation-community. The Spirit of Life holds everything together in that it enables the various creatures to live with each other, for each other and in each other, created through divine love and destined for eternal joy.[19]

What a significant way to express the richness of mutual human relationships, the beauty of living with, for, and in each other as a representation of the ultimate *perichoretic* divine eternal love and joy!

Catherine Mowry LaCugna

Catherine LaCugna brings a more specific insight to what is being developed in this section regarding the prophetic vocation of the community of faith in light of the relational and communal Triune God. She bases her argument on the assumption that community happens when persons are united in common life, in fellowship with each other. Her basis for this

19. Moltmann, "The Triune God: Rich in Relationships," 5. In order to expand the concept of "Base Communities," here is what Boff states: "The basic communities mean 'building a living church rather than multiplying material structures.' The communities are built on a more vital, lively, intimate participation in a more or less homogeneous entity, as their members seek to live the essence of the Christian message: the universal parenthood of God, communion with all human beings, the following of Jesus Christ who died and rose again, the celebration of the resurrection and the Eucharist, and the upbuilding of the kingdom of God, already under way in history as the liberation of the whole human being and all human beings. Christian life in the basic communities is characterized by the absence of alienating structures, by direct relationships, by reciprocity, by a deep communion, by mutual assistance by communality of gospel ideals, by equality among members" (see Boff, *Ecclesiogenesis*, 4).

argument is her view that, "God exists as three persons in communion, as communion which is the ground of every other type of communion."[20] For LaCugna, "the mysteries of human personhood and communion have their origin and destiny in God's personal existence."[21] Her approach to the social and relational character of human personhood is found in Trinitarian relational personhood. "Only in *communion* can God be what God is, and only as *communion* can God be at all."[22] This idea is transferable to human beings as well. A person is a person only in relation to others, in mutual relationality. As LaCugna affirms, "to exist as a person is to be referred to others."[23] It may seem obvious, but the theological principle for this claim comes from the Triune divine relationship of mutuality, *koinonia*. The theological dimension of this assertion is directly related to the assumption that the "person is neither autonomous nor heteronomous but theonomous," which bases human personhood in reference to "its origin and destiny in God."[24] Using LaCugna's approach, Ernest Byron Anderson helps us to better understand and appropriate these concepts. He says:

> It is here that we discover the impossibility of either a pure heteronomy, as a "naming oneself with reference to another," or a pure autonomy, as a "naming oneself with reference to oneself." Both of these options are destructive of persons through the domination and oppression of the first and the narcissism of the second. In the dance of the Trinity we find "persons in relation" named only as they can be, in reference to another who is also oneself in relation. It is here in the dance that we find the sources and reference for the truly "theonomous" self, a self "named with reference to its origin and destiny in God," an origin and destiny of relatedness to and with God.[25]

This postulation of theonomous personhood deconstructs the tendency toward self-sufficiency and individualism seen in present day society. The prophetic community as "theonomous community" is called to disrupt this tension and proclaim a genuine communion of humanity. LaCugna summarizes by saying that, "what matters is that we hold on to the assertion

20. LaCugna, *God for Us*, 259.

21. Ibid., 246.

22. Ibid., 260.

23. Ibid., 289.

24. Ibid., 290.

25. Anderson, *Worship and Christian Identity*, 148.

that God is personal, and that therefore the proper subject matter of the doctrine of the Trinity is the encounter between divine and human persons in the economy of redemption."[26] The prophetic community as "theonomous community" is called to disrupt this tension and proclaim a genuine communion of humanity.

ANALYSIS OF THE PRAYER: HOW PROPHETIC TRINITARIAN PRAYER STRENGTHS PROPHETIC COMMUNITY

Given this theological perspective from recent theologians characterized by their socio-political approaches to Trinitarian theology, I can now suggest a personal theological analysis using the prayer introduced above as a point of reference. My intention is to call upon the political sensitivity of the worshippers to take seriously the present reality of human social, political, and economic conditions, by employing the community of the triune God as the paradigm for Christian prophetic praxis in society.

Invocation is the main liturgical element in the Trinitarian prayer presented above. The imperative "come" in each one of the three stanzas follows the liturgical pattern of invocation prayers. The repetitive form "light of the world" is present only as an emphatic resource of language or figure of speech that well applies to each person of the Trinity affirming their unity and balanced level of significance.

The images of "Father" and "Son" are not present in this prayer. The reason for this is my conviction that neither the individual character of personality nor anthropomorphic subjectivity necessarily has significance for a prophetic Trinitarian paradigm. Holistic and *hypostatic* relationships better describe the essence of triune reciprocal communion. Boff proposes that we keep the term *perichoresis* central in the theological reflection on the relational Trinity, in which Trinitarian equilibrium is manifested "since all is triadic and perichoretically implied; all is shared, circulated, reciprocally received, united through communion."[27] According to Boff, this approach to the mystery of the Trinity offers an extremely rich suggestion in "the context of oppression and desire for liberation." He goes on to say:

---

26. LaCugna, *God for Us*, 305.
27. Boff, *Trinity and Society*, 6.

> The oppressed struggle for participation at all levels of life, for a just
> and egalitarian sharing while respecting the differences between
> persons and groups; they seek communion with other cultures
> and other values, and with God as the ultimate meaning of history
> and of their own hearts. As these realities are withheld from them
> in history, they feel obliged to undertake a process of liberation
> that seeks to enlarge the space for participation and communion
> available to them. For those who have faith, the trinitarian com-
> munion between the divine Three, the union between them in love
> and vital interpenetration, can serve as a source of inspiration, as
> a utopian goal that generates models of successively diminishing
> differences. This is one of the reasons why I am taking the concept
> of perichoresis as the structural axis of these thoughts. It speaks to
> the oppressed in their quest and struggle for integral liberation.[28]

The prophetic trinitarian paradigm, in holistic and *perichoretic* relationship, gives us the undeniable foundation for communion inviting everyone
and the whole universe to participate in the divine life as Jesus prayed, "May
they be one in us . . . that they may be one as we are one" (John 17:21–22).
As Anderson suggests, "perichoresis points to a way of life in and with
others that preserves distinctiveness without it becoming individualistic,
autonomous, or isolated. The Trinitarian grammar is a grammar about God
and person by which we name God and ourselves in and by our history of
relationship, or agency, with one another."[29]

The primary theological element present in the aforementioned prayer
is its Trinitarian structure. It is addressed to God, the Prophet of prophets;
to Jesus Christ, the Incarnate prophet; and to the Holy Spirit, the Spirit of
prophets. Thus, it addresses the Triune God as prophet, the ultimate source
for prophetic Christian action in the world.

The first image present in the prayer, "God, Prophet of prophets,"
provides a great challenge for anyone who seeks to be prophetic. God as a
reference for prophetic action does not present a simple, single paradigm
to follow. Nevertheless, as was mentioned before, it is only in close intimacy with God that a prophet is able to see the invisible through the light
of God's eyes. It also implies a close relationship to the world. This close
spiritual relationship with God and close commitment to the world are

28. Ibid., 6–7.

29. Anderson, *Worship and Christian Identity*, 144. For a clear definition of the Greek
term *perichoresis* (used by the eight century Greek theologian John Damascene), see
LaCugna, *God for Us*, 271.

the primary elements in prophetic activity. As Heschel reminds us, "The prophet's eye is directed to the contemporary scene; the society and its conduct are the main themes of his speeches. Yet his ear is inclined to God. He is a person struck by the glory and presence of God, overpowered by the hand of God. Yet his true greatness is his ability to hold God and man in a single thought."[30] It is a spirituality, as Karl Barth would say, that requires that one hold the Scripture in the one hand, and the newspaper in the other hand.[31] It is in the Scripture and in the contemporary events that prophets find guidance to denounce what is hidden before us. It is also a spirituality that recognizes the Triune God as the author and sustainer of the Word. The foundation for prophetic action in the world is the Scripture. Scripture is the lens that helps translucent eyes to see what is hidden, the source and reference for prophetic praxis.

The second image present in the prayer, "Jesus Christ, incarnate prophet," emphasizes the immanent presence of God (*theophany*). Jesus Christ's *epiphanic* immanence is the annunciation of all possibilities. The One who *has been sent* (Luke 4:18c) came to proclaim abundant life for all human beings. Jesus' incarnated ministry is the reference source for prophetic action in the world. Jesus' life, suffering, death, and resurrection—the paschal mystery—proclaims the redemption of humanity, the sacramental manifestation of social change. The paschal mystery isolated from the redemption of humanity would be simply rendered as one more mythical historical event and would lose the sacramental meaning of Christ's redemptive incarnation. Jesus Christ—incarnated prophet, the reference and author of the sacramental, who sees beyond all possibilities—is the paradigm for prophetic ministry seeking social transformation. Prophets are not alone. Their ultimate reference is the incarnate Jesus whose paschal mystery proclaims human redemption. Life for the community is their goal and self-offering. That is why the reference for prophets to proclaim human redemption is sacramental. Through sacramental praxis, prophets are encouraged to reclaim abundant life for all people.

The third image present in this prayer, "Holy Spirit, spirit of prophets" describes the energy that keeps alive every single prophetic action. The one who denounces injustices, aggressions, xenophobisms, and all sorts of

---

30. Heschel, *The Prophets*, 21.

31. This is a spirituality developed in the process of building a bridge between Scripture and the contemporary world. Karl Barth's famous dictum teaches us that to do theology we should take the Scripture in one hand and the newspaper in the other hand.

oppressions against children, women, men, races, cultures, and so-called minorities, has a political vision illuminated by the Holy Spirit. Prophets committed to transformation in the world find themselves engaged in a profound relationship with the Spirit who keeps them awake to see and to denounce all kinds of signs of obscurity in our midst. The ultimate goal of prophets, who embody the Spirit of prophets, is a living action, a mission— *"to bring good news to the poor . . . to proclaim release to the captives . . . to recovery of sight to the blind . . . to let the oppressed go free . . . and to proclaim the year of the Lord's favor"* (Luke 4:18b–19). That is why a key resource for prophets in anticipating transformation is ethics. The ethical sensitivity of prophets illuminates their path in denouncing the signs of oppression and anti-life around the world.

The prophetic vocation of the community of faith is to be shaped by the prophetic trinitarian divine community. The conceptual sense of the term *vocatio* suggested here is intentionally theological and ethical. The term is based on God's call for social transformation rooted in Christian action and focused on the common good. From that perspective, *vocatio* can be understood as the Christian response to God's call for the sake of the collective well-being.

THE TRINITARIAN STRUCTURE OF PROPHETIC ACTION AND VOCATION

In many aspects such an understanding of the prophetic vocation of the community of faith has invariably been neutralized. The established social, political, and economical systems have been the primary generator of this neutralization. In general, it is possible to notice many Christian communities as not perceiving and unaffected by the overwhelming problems facing the human species. The prophetic vocation of the church pushes the community to see, to assay, and to denounce concrete systems of evil that compromise the dignity of human beings.

As previously observed, the references for the prophetic vocation of the community of faith suggested here are Scripture, sacrament, and ethics.[32] The diagram below illustrates a Trinitarian approach to prophetic action and the structure of prophetic vocation.

---

32. I am drawing here on Chauvet's threefold structure of that which sustains Christian identity: Scripture, sacraments, and ethics. See Chauvet, *Symbol and Sacrament*, 172.

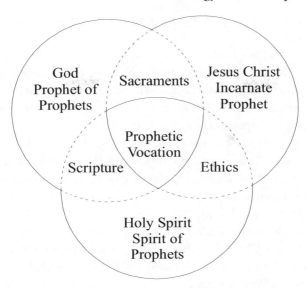

Based on a trinitarian concept, the structure of prophetic vocation that I suggest here is built mainly on three principles, which, as mentioned before, Chauvet describes as the "Structure of Christian Identity," and which for me sustains the prophetic vocation of the church: Scripture, sacraments, and ethics. This threefold structure has the *perichoretic* dimension of interconnection in which each depends on the other, and which could not be what it is without the coordinated phenomena of relationship to one another.

How does this structure function? Related to the position of God as Prophet of Prophets, in this Trinitarian structure, is "Scripture," where the Scripture is recognized as a gift from God, the source of inspiration for prophetic vocation as well as the ongoing manifestation of the Word. Christ's position is specified as "sacrament," in which the community of faith celebrates the sacraments as a memorial of Christ's paschal mystery, the chief paradigm for self-giving life. The Holy Spirit's position corresponds in this schema to "ethics," where brothers and sisters act in justice and mercy through the power of the presence of the Holy Spirit who gives strength and vigor for prophetic praxis. Thus, a community of faith with a prophetic vocation would believe: (1) that the Scripture is the living Word of God for us today; (2) that liturgical and sacramental celebrations reclaim memory of the life, death, and resurrection of Jesus Christ; and (3) that

73

Christian human ethics, personal or communal, is inspired by the work of the Holy Spirit.

The practical implication for this structure of prophetic vocation is the possibility for it to legitimate and revitalize the community's faith, identity and mission. First, the social-historical-cultural character of Scripture plays an inevitable role in the community's faith. The reverse operates on the same level of importance, that is, the celebrating praxis of the Christian community emphasizes the epistemological character of the Scripture. Chauvet declares, "the community writes itself in the book it reads."[33] He also affirms that, "Book and community are recognized as inseparable. The book is nothing without the community, and the community finds in the book the mirror of its identity."[34]

Second, the sacramentality of the church becomes central as the liturgical expression of Christ's paschal mystery. The Christian community will grow in faith when the whole meaning of the sacramental celebration is conceived as repeating the gestures, words, and self-giving life of the Risen One in prophetic memory of him. It is through the sacraments that Christ greets us, reveals his paschal mystery, assures God's promised blessings, and affirms the presence of the Holy Spirit, in which can be found all we need to accomplish prophetic action. There can be no possibility of prophetic vocation without the sacraments of the Church. Indeed, the sacraments are channels of prophetic call. They are place and space for prophetic covenant renewal. The sacraments bring to prophets the passionate way to live and to make life in the world, created and sustained by the One who makes life a gift for all.

Third, ethics is a basic part of the Christian mission, where the prophetic vocation is expressed in a 'life of witness,' both ethical witness and ethical praxis. As Enrique Dussel pointed out, "the ethical consists in praxis. It consists in praxis as activity directed toward, and relationship to, the other as other, as person, as sacred, as absolute."[35] As Christians, we have an important mission in our history in which the gap between rich and poor, developed and developing world, health and disease, and freedom and subordination reaches a scandalous level that requires urgent prophetic and ethical responses. A prophetic-oriented ethic can make God's promised kingdom a reality in our time. As Moltmann suggests, "To act ethically in

33. Ibid., 209.
34. Ibid.
35. Dussel, *Ethics and Community*, 49.

a Christian sense means to participate in God's history in the midst of our own history, to integrate ourselves into the comprehensive process of God's liberation of the world, and to discover our own role in this according to our own calling and abilities."[36] It is in acting out God's love, doing mission, that Christians express the ultimate meaning of their own prophetic vocation. A more extensive argument on the structure of prophetic vocation will be developed in chapter four through what I call a "matrix of total sacramental rituality."

TRANSFORMATIVE POTENTIAL OF LITURGICAL PRAXIS: CHURCH AND WORLD

It is assumed that a community of faith, engaged in prophetic praxis, has the potential to disclose, from the perspective of the human sciences, not only the transcendent and spiritual meaning of its existence, but also the relevance of its praxis as a vehicle of transformation in society. Indeed, the prophetic celebrating community can be an agency of proclamation and a prophetic voice that cries out liberation from all kinds of situations in which human beings lose their dignity, a sign of commitment with and for the whole created world. To achieve this goal, some parameters must be taken into consideration. A question, then, undergirds the need for investigation: What are the foundational socio-religious-cultural elements that members of the Church need to conceive, process, and assimilate in order to be agents of transformation through liturgical practices?

This section is meant to explore the meaning of and possibilities for the celebrating community in such a way that it may find strength and courage to act and to profess its vocation toward transformation for the inhabited world—*oikoumene*. Given the *oikoumene* frame of reference, the cosmological *sitz im leben* for transformative praxis, some prerogatives must be considered. A community that seeks transformation must be open to reading and reflecting upon issues surrounding (1) its relationship to the world; (2) the language of its liturgical life; and (3) its immersion into diverse cultural contexts. These issues are the pillars that sustain the focus on transformation. The community of faith needs to build its transformative project based on social-religious-cultural parameters, assuming its responsibility for social justice, religious commitment, and cultural receptivity. These three dimensions (social, religious, and cultural), as foundational

36. Moltmann, *On Human Dignity*, 111.

elements that support transformation, suggest a sequence of alternative themes around which a dialogue on the transformative potential of the liturgical praxis emerges. They are: Church and world, liturgical language, and socio-cultural contexts. These three represent the core references for the transformative potential of liturgical praxis that I now want to explore.

We, members of the Church, need to recognize that we are living in an era of global interconnections. Globalization is the central reality of today's world. Anyone who has even minor access to media of communication is aware of the emerging worldwide interconnection. Something that happens somewhere else in the world can be known rapidly, indeed, as it is occurring, such as the tragic earthquake and tsunami in Japan; the uprising that led to the ousting of Mubarak in Egypt; the Katrina tragedy in New Orleans; the uprising in Syria, etc. Whether related to religion, economic, social, political or cultural issues, the effects of such things can deeply affect every human class. Indeed, as Martin Luther King, Jr. said, whatever affects one person or group anywhere in the world affects all persons—including God—directly or indirectly. This is so because God has created a thoroughly relational creation. King said that "as nations and individuals, we are interdependent."[37] And then famously he said: "It really boils down to this: that all life is interrelated. We are all caught up in an inescapable network of mutuality, tied into a single garment of destiny. Whatever affects one directly, affects all indirectly. We are made to live together because of the interrelated structure of reality."[38] The theological metaphor for this concept is that we all live under the same big roof—the big house—*oikoumene*.

This reminds us of the unequivocal universal socio-political fact that we are living together in a big house—*oikos*—which constitutes, as David Verner has pointed out, "the basic social-political unity."[39] Seeing *oikía / oikos* as the basic social-political unity of the world demands a realization that for Christians the source of this way of thinking about the basic social-political unity is theological, meaning that the God of the Hebrew prophets and Jesus Christ is the foundation. Indeed, Hebrew Bible scholar Terence E. Fretheim argues convincingly that throughout the First Testament we get a clear sense of the deeply communal or interdependent character of creation, as well as the "fundamentally *relational* understanding of the way in

37. King Jr., "A Christmas Sermon on Peace," in *The Trumpet of Conscience*, 68.
38. Ibid., 69.
39. Verner, *The Household of God*, 28.

which God acts in the world."[40] On this view, reality is fundamentally social or relational. God created the world such that interrelatedness is basic. The point is further affirmed by Fretheim when he asserts: "Each created entity is in symbiotic relationship with every other and in such a way that any act reverberates out and affects the whole, shaking this web with varying degrees of intensity."[41] This metaphor compels us to realize that our focus, as transformative community, is the kingdom-house of God: the global household, *oikoumene*, the whole inhabited earth, the world.[42] The imperative goal is the realization of, as Dussel calls it, "the community of the reign of God," which cannot be accomplished except by those "covenanted" as servant.[43] As Dussel sees it, this community "holds all things in 'common' (*koina*)," established "in the face-to-face of unity." According to Dussel, "in community, all individuals are persons for one another. Their relationships are 'practical,' and this praxis is that of the love that is charity: each serves the other for the other, in the friendship of all persons in all things . . . The community is the real, concrete agent and mover of history. In the community we are 'at home,' in safety and security, 'in common.'"[44] This goal is still ahead of us as a "not yet," but always pointing towards that horizon that reminds us: "There is much more to be done!" This is the challenge and task for all of us who are engaged in liturgy committed to transformation and justice: whoever is struggling for justice is also struggling for the kingdom of God.

The Greek term *oikoumene* also evokes the concept of universality. It addresses the inalienable desire for the unity of the Church, of the world, of creation, and of the people of God. It refers to the place where we all live, the household of all, as the Psalmist says, "The earth (*oikoumene*) is the Lord's and all that is in it, the world and those who live in it" (Ps 24:1). As

40. Fretheim, *God and World in the Old Testament*, 163. Fretheim powerfully develops this theme throughout the book, not least in chapter 6.

41. Ibid., 19.

42. Irvin affirms that the term *oikoumene*—a Greek word "emerged among the ancient churches following the conversion of the Roman Emperor Constantine the Great in 314 A.D." He continues saying that "the political-cultural meaning of *oikoumene* (literally the 'inhabited earth') of the Apostolic period, which coincided with the world of human culture known to the writers of the Second Testament (understood predominantly but not exclusively as the world of Greco-Roman culture), gave way to an ecclesiastical understanding of *oikoumene* represented by the hierarchy of the church and often under imperial domination" (see Irvin, *Hearing Many Voices*, 14).

43. Dussel, *Ethics and Community*, 45–46.

44. Ibid., 11.

Michael H. Crosby affirms: "Just as the social institution of kinship based in the *oikía* / *oikos* demanded concern for the well-being of all its members, so now, the social institution of post-industrial capitalism demands concern for the *oikoumene* and the preservation of ecological balance as well. What is needed is a new kind of household order based in justice that will help our entrance into the third millennium."[45] Transforming liturgy encounters its place in the concept of *oikoumene*, where those who seek unity join together in prophetic celebration to liberate, to build, to plant, and to edify together a peaceful world, a more just and more humane world, a world which is reconciling the human being with the Triune God, with itself, and with the entire creation. As implicit in the concept of *oikoumene*, recognizing a household of all and for all is one of the great challenges for transformation that a community of faith faces in this era of globalization.

Community life, above anything else, must retain respect for individuality as a prerequisite for respecting the collectivity, and vice versa. The individual has no meaning apart from the communal. As previously mentioned in Chapter One, Archbishop Desmond Tutu reminds us that we can be people only among other people. In order to be a human being at all, we need other human beings. "I am because other people are," Tutu writes. He also says: "The solitary, isolated human being is really a contradiction in terms . . . The totally self-sufficient person, if ever there could be one, is subhuman."[46] Tutu's concept of interrelatedness is based on the African principle of *ubuntu*. In any event, transformative liturgy should demonstrate its commitment to establishing the primacy of communal life. Whoever is defending communal interaction or integration, *oikoumene*, certainly is also fighting against the prevalence of wild xenophobia and insensate sectarianism in Church and world.[47]

Community happens when individuals live lives that are directed towards the other. As Martin Buber sees it, "community is the being no longer side by side but with one another of a multitude of persons. And this multitude, though it also moves towards one goal, yet experiences

45. Crosby, *House of Disciples*, 243–44.

46. Tutu, *God Has A Dream*, 25.

47. For an extensive reference on *oikoumene* as "social interaction" to the level of language, culture, ethnicity, and civilization, see Malina who says: "Social integration is rooted in directly embodied and/or particularized mutuality of persons in social contact . . . People grouped in ethnic entities eventually considered each other part of a common *oikoumene*, the inhabited 'household' world" (see Malina, *The Social Gospel of Jesus*, 79–80).

everywhere a turning to, a dynamic facing of, the other, a flowing from *I* to *Thou*. Community is where community happens."[48] The challenge we face when we worship through transformative liturgy is that we are called to think communally. A transformative liturgy has the potential to remind us to put communal necessities before individual preferences.

The attempt to discern and understand the relationship between the Church and the World, from the perspective presented up to this point, is an extremely demanding task. It is demanding precisely because the necessary methodological approach is that of dialectical reflection between both the ontologically existential and the epistemologically critical. Even though it is possible to discuss and understand this dialectic from a strictly theological perspective, to be most effective, one needs to use different lenses and methodologies, which will reveal incursions into a constructive interdisciplinary foundation.

To comprehend the ontological relationship between the Church and the world, we must start with the assimilation of the language of social body. The theme of the Church as Christ's Body, a social body, was briefly explored in Chapter Two. Nonetheless, we must return to it precisely because the "Body" is a crucial metaphor for political, economic, and social analysis, and this is central for a responsible theological examination of the relationship between Church and world.

To participate in the Church is to believe in its institution as Christ's body, the visible sign of God's redemptive project for the world. This is the condition for Christian existence: participation as members of a true institutional body—the Body of Christ, where individual integrity is directly related to social dignity. These aspects cannot be separated from each other. The theological ground for this assertion is the Body of Christ as social body, the Church, the community of the baptized. It expresses the ultimate level of individual integrity for the sake of social dignity. William Cavanaugh calls our attention to the fact that "the unfaithfulness of the church in the present age is based to some extent precisely on its failure to take itself seriously as the continuation of Christ's body in the world and to conform itself, body and soul, not to the world but to Christ (Rom 12:2)."[49] The reality is that the Church is the body of Christ and thus has the irrefutable responsibility to be Christ's body in history, offering itself as the

---

48. Buber, *Between Man and Man*, 31.
49. Cavanaugh, *Torture and Eucharist*, 233.

visible body of Christ as an agent of transformation and reconciliation of the world.

Cavanaugh's methodology is both political and ecclesiological. Accordingly, it is essential to recognize and to assimilate the language of social body. Cavanaugh helps us to understand that, on the one hand, the true body of Christ (*corpus verum*) is the suffering body, the body that is tortured and sacrificed. On the other hand, "the Church is the body of Christ because it performs an *anamnesis* of Christ's sacrifice. The true body of Christ is the suffering body, the destitute body, the body which is tortured and sacrificed."[50] It reflects the meaning of solidarity. As Cavanaugh points out, the "Eucharist demands that true unity be achieved, that people overcome alienation from each other and become reconciled, caring for each other, especially the weak, in community and solidarity."[51] Through prophetic actions in the world, the church becomes visible when it acts in solidarity with the suffering of humanity.

Based on this perspective, I contend that the Church is called to recognize its own fragility and to understand itself as the visible body of Christ present in the world, a body that suffered and still suffers through the insane human actions against both individuals and the collective social body. Violence against the human body is violence against Christ. The issue here is not just to denounce those who promote the *pathos* of humanity, but also to point out the outrageous political and economical systems that, hidden through the image of "the developed ones," dignify signs of anti-life throughout the world.

Gutiérrez's methodological approach to the relationship between Church and world is certainly an ideological one, and one which has a clear political connotation. From the standpoint of a specific Latin American context, his theology is based on the suffering of God's people, especially the poor. Gutiérrez's account in relating Church and world is ideological because it has political implications and radical commitment against the *status quo*. He says: "If theological reflection does not vitalize the action of the Christian community in the world by making its commitment to charity fuller and more radical, if—more concretely—in Latin America it does not lead the Church to be on the side of the oppressed classes and dominated peoples, clearly and without qualifications, then this theological reflection will have been of little value. Worse yet, it will have served only to

50. Ibid., 267.
51. Ibid., 268.

justify half-measures and ineffective approaches and to rationalize a departure from the Gospel."[52] The historical presence of the Church in the world has "an inescapable political dimension."[53] It is my understanding that the Church must take into consideration its historical political presence in the world. As a sign of God's presence and action in the world, the Church finds its meaning and vocation on the basis of an effective consciousness of the world and a concrete commitment to it. The Church does not belong to the world but is renewed and transformed by the challenges of the world. As a community of faith we need to turn to the world where God, Christ and the Holy Spirit are present and active.

SOCIO-CULTURAL CONTEXTS

It is not surprising that the majority of ordinary people in the Church are not familiar with the important contributions of the socio-cultural fields in the liturgical studies arena. Actually, this happens not only with the regular "lay" people but also with a considerable number of clergy. For them, the social sciences (sociology, anthropology, political science, economics, etc.) have nothing to do with their Christian faith, life, and praxis. For such people, spirituality and worship are empirically experienced. In other words, they are formed by pragmatic oral tradition. In that sense, for the majority of ordinary people of the church, science, which comes from reason, has no connection with faith, which comes from heart and spirit. This kind of reluctance to approach the social sciences and all of the related subjects, including the concept of culture, suggests some interesting issues to think about in terms of the relationship between social sciences and liturgy. This is not simply a matter of sociological or anthropological investigation. It has to do with theology and liturgy as well.

The social sciences, especially sociology and anthropology, provide excellent instruments for social analysis. These critical and analytical tools are not beyond the limits of the church's context. With the mediation of the social sciences and a responsible theological discernment, it is possible to envision culturally creative liturgical praxis s where that which is essential is retained and the new is welcomed, in order to legitimate and eternalize sound community spiritual praxis.

52. Gutiérrez, *A Theology of Liberation*, 174.
53. Ibid., 32.

Mary Collins, in her book *Worship: Renewal to Practice*, affirms that the church "must have mechanisms for enabling creativity to effect institutional change or for inhibiting such an outcome."[54] She says that while this process of changing does not come without destabilization, it has the potential to reveal meaning in the tradition. Collins continues:

> Does this attempt to reorder the world of common public meaning allow the community to see and to absorb a new vision and yet to keep a firm grasp on the common tradition? The community will inevitably suffer a measure of destabilization as it is confronted with the unfamiliar. But if the new insight originally born through the individual psyche's creative achievement has power to reveal meaning latent in the tradition, it will stimulate emotional, intellectual, aesthetic and moral response from others within the community. As that broadened base of response signals a valuable augmentation of the tradition, others will take it up, even promote it, and the social group will have moved a step closer to sanctioning the gain as a public achievement.[55]

The process of transformation demands conversion to the new or unknown, and a clear response to foundational questions such as: Are the new creative liturgical praxis comprehensible to the community? Do they speak to the hearts and minds of the majority of the community's celebrants? Are they valuable to the life of the community and the society at large? Are they challenging the community's commitment to participating in the world as Christ's body, a body in search of socio-economic transformation? The process of changing does not happen overnight or without suffering "a measure of destabilization," as Collins has suggested. What the Church needs is to experience the process of changing critically and responsibly in order to learn from its mistakes as well as from its most expressive and authentic praxis. The process takes time and discernment.

The substance of the question is how the community of faith can immerse itself into social, political, economic, religious, and cultural issues in order to recognize the signs of our time and to engage in prophetic acts, renewing itself while seeking transformation. In other words, the whole process of transforming and being transformed requires from the community an awareness of the Christian historical trajectory, a consciousness of

54. Collins, *Worship*, 241.
55. Ibid., 241–42.

its cultural unity, and attentiveness to the transformative resonance of the Christian liturgical praxis in the world.

A transformative liturgy is not disconnected from cultural forces. To engage in socio-cultural issues is not to abandon the liturgical life of the church nor vice-versa. A liturgical celebration engendered by socio-cultural sensitivity and sustained by coherent theological meaning has in itself the potential for transformation. By "socio-cultural" I mean a complex system of behavior, belief, and language patterns of a given social group, in which concepts and specific systems of symbolic meaning are achieved, apprehended, and applied, in a cyclical, mutual, and dynamic process of living and learning. It has a close parallel to most textbook and anthropological definitions of "culture," which usually express roughly the same concept in different ways. The more complex a term is, the less consensus there is about its meaning. "Culture" and "socio-cultural" in this section are used interchangeably. I would say that culture is simply a result of a matrix of relationships in a given human group. Even though this is a brief definition, it includes the necessary components, under the term "matrix of relationships," which encompasses social, political, economic, religious, artistic, and philosophical practice and assumptions of a given social group. An appropriate question for the conversation on this matter would be: "What are the resources for a prophetic "culturally rooted" liturgical praxis?"

Clifford Geertz, in *The Interpretation of Culture*, says that the concept of culture is polysemic, a sort of "theoretical diffusion," as he defines it. For Geertz, culture refers to: "(1) the total way of life of a people; (2) the social legacy the individual acquires from his group; (3) a way of thinking, feeling, and believing; (4) an abstraction from behavior; (5) a theory on the part of the anthropologist about the way in which a group of people in fact behave; (6) a store-house of pooled learning; (7) a set of standardized orientations to recurrent problems; (8) learned behavior; (9) a set of techniques for adjusting both to the external environment and to other men; (10) a precipitate of history."[56] As seen in this matrix of different approaches, the concept of culture is essentially a semiotic one, and as such, needs to be appropriated in its complex language discourse. In Geertz, the description for this concept is located in the minds and hearts of humankind.[57] This means that multifaceted forms of signs and symbols express it. That is why he says: "Culture is most effectively treated purely as a symbolic system, by isolating

56. Geertz, *The Interpretation of Cultures*, 4–5.

57. Ibid., 5 and 11.

its elements, specifying the internal relationships among those elements, and then characterizing the whole system in some general way—according to the core symbols around which it is organized, the underlying structures of which it is a surface expression, or the ideological principles upon which it is based."[58] Religion is not separate from this cyclical system process. It is a cyclical system precisely because the religious experiences are usually presented, assimilated, and passed on as relevant symbolic concepts. In sum, as Geertz suggests, without humankind, there is no culture; and without culture, there is no humankind. It is a learning process upon which concepts and specific systems of symbolic meaning are attained, apprehended, and applied, in a cyclical process, and in a given cultural context. A liturgy that is "culturally rooted" needs to understand and recognize this cyclical system.

Anscar J. Chupungco, in his book *Cultural Adaptation of the Liturgy*, introduces a necessary approach for bringing cultural dimension to liturgy. According to him, "Liturgical renewal has also to address itself to the question of liturgical adaptation to various cultures."[59] In his understanding, "liturgical adaptation is the admission into the liturgy of elements of culture and traditions, which through the process of purification can serve as vehicles of the liturgy for the utility or need of a particular cultural group."[60] The process of liturgical adaptation is a complex task that involves a number of fields. It does not happen unilaterally. As Chupungco rightly observes, "theology, exegesis, sociology, anthropology, psychology, linguistics and the arts."[61] Chupungco's theological reference for this assertion is the event of the incarnation. The centrality of the incarnation provides the Christian understanding with a theological foundation for socio-cultural adaptation of worship. "In the final analysis," Chupungco writes, "the mystery of the incarnation is the theological principle of adaptation. The Word of God, in assuming the condition of man, except sin, bound himself to the history, culture, traditions and religion of his own people."[62] The immanence of the divine among human beings provides the theological paradigm for cultural sensitivity.

---

58. Ibid., 17.
59. Chupungco, *Cultural Adaptation of the Liturgy*, 1.
60. Ibid., 48.
61. Ibid., 53.
62. Ibid., 58.

One cannot help but appreciate Chupungco's theory, particularly his valuable differentiation between three types of liturgical adaptation: (1) *accomodatio*; (2) acculturation; and (3) inculturation.[63] For my purpose, it is sufficient to say that the last two terms are related to culture and Chupungco summarizes their differences by saying, "While acculturation induces a change or modification of the Roman genius through the assumption of new cultural elements, inculturation brings about a change in the culture through the entry of the Christian message. The latter process is a form of conversion to the faith, a metanoia of pre-Christian rites."[64]

In their book *Making Room at the Table*, Brian K. Blount and Lenora T. Tisdale address the topic of worship and culture with special attention to the celebration of the Eucharist. They provide a broad definition of culture as multi-realities that locate and identify who we are and what we believe and value. They use the term culture "to mean the social, linguistic, national, ethnic, and theological realities that locate and identify who we are and what we believe and value."[65] This perspective emphasizes the social aspect of culture, not unlike my appropriation and incorporation of the term "socio-cultural," a term that is particularly appropriate to use in a liturgical context, and in discussions on transformative liturgy. For me, it reflects the understanding that the community of faith, inserted in temporal realities, and confronting multicultural engagements inside and outside the church, is called to explore its liturgical praxis as means of multicultural challenges of inclusion, and to acknowledge the role of the entire community as an agent of a sound socio-cultural affirmation.

Geddes W. Hanson brings to the conceptual dialogue between culture and organization a concept of culture-organization relationship that could well be applied to the culture-church relationship. As Hanson affirms, "the examination of the issue of 'multicultural' worship will proceed from this perspective on the culture-organization relation."[66] In the framework of this point of view, Hanson emphasizes a metaphorical analysis of the organization as a culture. She says: In a partial reverting to the classical roots of the word, the organization can be viewed as a plant, in the sense that it exists to bear particular fruit. The fruit of the collective, which can be understood

---

63. Ibid., 81–86. For more in depth approaches on the matter, see Chupungco, *Liturgical Inculturation*; and Chupungco, *Worship: Beyond Inculturation*.

64. Chupungco, *Cultural Adaptation of the Liturgy*, 84.

65. Blount and Tisdale, ed., *Making Room at the Table*, ix.

66. Hanson, "'Multicultural' Worship: A Careful Consideration," 148–49.

as political, intellectual, economic, social, artistic, or religious artifacts, take the shape they do because they are fruit of that particular vine. To the degree that there is "cultural integrity," the fruit on every branch grows out of common commitments to the particular values that the culture exists to embody.[67] The church, especially through its liturgy, represents this plant that bears cultural fruit. The question is, "What type of cultural fruit has been cultivated in our church." Furthermore, "What are the essences of this cultural fruit?"

From a prophetic perspective, the challenge before us is to make our living liturgical praxis an effective ground of socio-cultural manifestations that affirm the community's commitment to make this world a better place for every human being. We need prophetic liturgical praxis enriched by socio-cultural principles so that we can expand our horizons for new liturgical possibilities, possibilities that will challenge the social-political-economic system, and not the contrary. What we have seen in our society is a subliminal inversion of this principle. In other words, the social-political-economic system is transforming the liturgy, which is unacceptable from the prophetic perspective. The question at stake is how the celebrating community could be able to understand its own *sitz im leben* (its social, political, economical, religious, and cultural systems), in order to recognize dialectically the signs of good and evil, life and death, and to act critically and prophetically, renewing itself while envisioning "the possibility that our children's children will learn at last to live as a community among community."[68] The whole process of celebrating together under such an assumption will facilitate the community's awareness of the Christian historical trajectory and a consciousness of its cultural unity, with attentiveness to the transformative resonance of the Christian liturgical praxis in the world.

LITURGY AND SOCIO-ECONOMIC JUSTICE

In this section, I try to make sense of the claim that prophetic liturgy can be effective mediation, which contributes to the establishment of socio-economic justice. Within this broader topic, I will focus specifically on the contributions of liturgical scholars who have significant insights that corroborate this claim. I also want to focus on particular issues that describe and critique the liturgical praxis of the Church in light of its socio-economic

67. Ibid., 148.

68. Daly, Cobb, and Cobb, *For the Common Good*, 400.

understanding.[69] Although special attention will be given to my own social and ecclesial location, namely, the Brazilian Methodist context, my aim is to provide a general critique of the liturgical praxis of the Church, regardless of context. Two simple questions, already raised in the introduction to this chapter, will help to focus the conversation: What are the contributions of the prophetic liturgy as a mediation of socio-economic transformation of unjust systems? Does liturgy generally have anything to do with socio-economic justice?

It is necessary to begin by elucidating the use of socio-economic science as a referential element for this discussion. Walter Owensby, in his book *Economics for Prophets*, presents the following definition: "economics is the study of the principles by which society organizes itself to use scarce resources for the production and distribution of goods and services."[70] At first glance, economics might seem to have no connections with liturgy. Actually, the tendency is to see economics as a distant academic discipline. Owensby makes the further claim that, "every economic decision changes the world—not only the world that is, but the world that will be. There are no pure economic realities because economic realities are also social realities . . . [S]ince economic decisions have moral effects, it is not only acceptable but inescapable that economists, policymakers, and citizens function with a particular set of values and a vision of a preferred future."[71] Thus, it is not only acceptable, but in fact inescapable, to recognize that economics does have something to do with liturgy, and vice-versa. They both have ethical implications. Constructive dialogue between liturgy and socio-economics will provide the basic framework for an analysis of the present time. The field of socio-economics should be considered as one possible referential instrument for a transforming and engaging Christian community committed to social justice. Therefore, as I will point out, we can find a variety of possibilities to bring together key elements from contemporary liturgical theology, and which also contributes to understanding the relationship between liturgy and socio-economics. Not all liturgical

69. I am referring to liturgical praxis in its fullness. That is, in all correlated concepts present in its meaning, including liturgical theology, sacramental theology, liturgical language, ritual, etc. Some authors emphasize the relationship between social, political, economic justice and liturgy; others, the sacramental life of the Church; yet others, ritual praxis and its variety of languages. My methodology reflects a matrix of understanding that is informed by all these.

70. Owensby, *Economics for Prophets*, xiii.

71. Ibid., xv.

theology scholars bring both fields together, but with careful examination from some of them, a dialogue can happen.

In this case, the problem is not related to language issues. It is not a situation where they cannot communicate with each other. From my point of view, the problem is methodological and pedagogical. It has to do with political strategies. Both fields need to dialogue more often, searching for responsible ways to create interaction between common key elements that promote a more engaged Christian praxis in the world. The implication of this assumption is that other elements are also needed—from the social sciences, for example—in order to dig deeply into the meaning of the liturgy, in general, and the meaning of the sacraments, in particular, as sources and paradigms for social justice.

One of Romano Guardini's most startling assertions is that, "The liturgy has no purpose, or, at least, it cannot be considered from the standpoint of purpose. It is not a means which is adapted to attain a certain end—it is an end in itself."[72] He makes this point by comparing the purpose of liturgy to child's play, declaring: "Such is the wonderful fact which the liturgy demonstrates; it unites art and reality in a supernatural childhood before God . . . These forms are the vital expression of real and frankly supernatural life. But this has one thing in common with the play of the child and the life of art—it has no purpose, but it is full of profound meaning. It is not work, but play."[73] From Guardini's perspective, the very purpose of the liturgy is "to understand simplicity in life," and to play "the divinely ordained game of the liturgy in liberty and beauty and holy joy before God."[74] The key element here, for a living liturgical life sensitive to the socio-economic demands of this world, is how to accomplish this wonderful dream in such a postmodern society as ours, where the "unprofitable," to use Guardini's word, the disposable, and "feeling good" is about to take (or has already taken) the place of the liturgy in the church. The socio-economic order is silently introducing a language of "wants" into the church, which is creating an entirely new lexicon for liturgy. As has been suggested, economics deals with wants, not needs. I would suggest that we take cues from these critiques and observations, and strive to maintain simplicity in life, playing the divinely ordained game of the liturgy with the eyes, ears, mouths, and minds of prophets, which surely will help us think and speak what liturgy

72. Guardini, "The Playfulness of the Liturgy," 41.

73. Ibid., 43.

74. Ibid., 44.

is about, impelling us to replace the goal of "feeling good" of the socio-economic system with God's project for all peoples: the triumph of justice.

Schmemann also talks about the joyful component of the liturgy. For him, the church, from its inception, has been both the source and the fulfillment of joy. In his eyes, the Eucharist is the sacrament of joy. "We have no other means of entering into that joy, no way of understanding it, except through the one action which from the beginning has been for the Church both the source and the fulfillment of joy, the very sacrament of joy, the Eucharist."[75] From this perspective of understanding the Eucharist as a "procession into the kingdom," we are compelled to go forth with joy, proclaiming the restoration of love, peace, and justice as the very life of the world. In this way, the sacramental celebration has no end. It continues on in our return to the world, the time of the church, the time of salvation and redemption. The key element here is the possibility given to humankind to see in and through the world the kingdom of God, where joy, peace, love, justice, and equality is given through Christ's paschal mystery so that, in this joy, we may challenge all human plans that are not in conformity with Christ, who is the life of the world. In a prophetic sense, this happens when sacramental praxis embodies signs of life and gestures of change. The challenge before us is to find a way to embody theological themes in our complex Christian way of celebrating the sacraments, while at the same time remaining faithful to our mission of being agents of love, justice and restoration. According to Schmemann, all of this depends on our being authentic witnesses of that joy: the joy that comes from the Holy Spirit, which ushers new life into the world.

Anscar Chupungco tells us that liturgical theology needs to assess its direct connection to the political, economic, and cultural aspects of the worshipping community, the context in which that particular community is living, its existential place. Chupungco's reference point for the relationship between liturgy and social sciences is based on his description of the concept of "contextualization." He says: "Since in some parts of the world human oppression is the dominant feature of daily life, the context in which the local Church lives and works is deeply affected by the struggle for political, economic, and cultural freedom. In such places 'contextualization' is used to signify efforts toward liberation . . . In a sense, contextualization is allied with Christianity's prophetic role."[76] Among the many terms Chu-

75. Schmemann, *For the Life of the World*, 25.
76. Chupungco, *Liturgical Inculturation*, 19, 21.

89

pungco uses, it seems that "contextualization" is the one that has the closest connection to both prophetic and socio-economic issues. It refers to the process of taking the Gospel's liberating message and expressing it in terms that the "locals" can understand, by applying language and concepts that are close and familiar to their contextual situation.

Another important contribution of Chupungco's relates to the implications of a liturgy committed to theological, social, and political consciousness of the Church. He puts it this way:

> Questions have been raised regarding the openness of the liturgy to the theological, social and political climate existing in particular churches. Should not the liturgy, for example, use the language of liberation, in order to impress on the people the urgency of social and political reforms? Thus some experimenters incorporate liberation skits in the Mass as a form of liberation catechesis. It is obvious that a good liturgy has to reflect the experience of the community, or, to use a current expression, it must be relevant. Relevance, however, should be subject to certain conditions. The liturgy is not a forum for the propagation of the social and political ideologies, however Christian these may be in orientation. Indeed, it is only after the community has been imbued with that that the liturgy can admit them as elements of prayer. A "liberation liturgy" can only mean that the people's aspiration for liberation has been assumed by the Church into the reality of worship. Although such a liturgy will be influenced by the ideology and language of the movement, it will have to be rooted in the Word of God and centered on the Christian mystery.[77]

The "doing" of liturgical praxis mandates a practical dimension of the celebrating community, one where the subjective spiritual world is not disconnected from the concrete living world. In other words, the whole process of "doing" liturgy, under the previously presented assumption, will facilitate a coming together of the community's awareness of the Christian historical trajectory, consciousness of its own cultural unity, and attentiveness to the transformative resonance of Christian liturgical praxis in the world.

David Power explores a similar idea of Christians as witnesses in the world. For him, the living witness of believers and disciples complements the Eucharist. Sacramental practices embody an ethical ideal. He states:

> The relation between ethics and Eucharist can be looked at from two angles, each approach complementing the other. On the one

---

77. Chupungco, *Cultural Adaptation of the Liturgy*, 65–66.

hand, Eucharist embodies an ethical ideal that Christians are in turn expected to embody in their lives . . . How the ethical ideal is drawn from the sacrament says much to how the sacrament itself is understood to represent Christ and the Church. On the other hand, the ethics or praxis of a community bespeaks how well it has appropriated what is eucharistically expressed. Thus it may serve to offer a critique of the manner in which the church celebrates and understands what is celebrated in the sacrament. In the course of church history, the intersection of the order of justice and of the order of charity has been envisaged and acted out in different ways. At any given time it is of interest to Eucharistic theology to look for a relation between the ethical paradigm relating these two and the approaches taken to the celebration and explanation of the Eucharist . . . Another important ethical consideration has to do with the inclusion of the socially, personally, and religiously marginalized, and with the ways in which Eucharist fosters the appropriation of suffering into an ethical vision of the world.[78]

As we see in Power's sacramental theology (I would call it a social-sacramental theology), an ethical ideal reveals how the community of faith understands and appropriates the deep meaning of the sacrament itself, which, above all, evokes a praxis of love and justice which includes the socially, politically, and economically excluded in society. For Power, ethical presuppositions and consequences must go beyond the task of sacramental theology. They must be related to a social-political-economic enterprise. In this way, sacramental theology finds connections that link it to the living world. Power's assumptions about the sacramental celebrations of the Church bear a close relationship with the prophetic dimensions of the liturgy. He points out and argues against empty ritual language that is not tied to the divine promises of liberation or a freedom that faces the powers head-on. For Power, this cannot be a freedom which ignores a person's need; but rather, it must be a freedom that gives birth to a confidence which will bring about creative participation in building a better life for human beings. The key element inherent in this understanding is an appreciation of the role of the Holy Spirit in the sacramental practices. The Spirit evokes freedom; the Spirit *is* freedom. The community, empowered by the Holy Spirit, captures both the suffering and the hope of human beings, connecting them with the event of Christ's liberating paschal mystery, which is the language of God's self-giving love.

78. Power, *The Eucharistic Mystery*, 18.

James L. Empereur and Christopher G. Kiesling calls our attention to an engaging spirituality that presupposes a deep understanding of living in community, which necessarily implies, by the transforming acts of the Spirit, prophetic participation in the mission of the Church. This mission has its roots in liturgical celebration. They say, "If action for social justice is united with liturgical celebration, there is all the more reason to expect that our eyes will be opened to social justice implications of liturgy that we had not notice before."[79] Liturgical celebrations can be fertile grounds that germinate lives committed to socio-economic justice. One of the challenges we face as prophetic community of faith seeking socio-economic justice, is to overcome human oppression, the state in which many members of Christ's Body currently live. Empereur and Kiesling contend that one of the possible ways to overcome this critical social situation is to recognize that:

> The church's mission as sacrament to the world requires that it often be prophetic and counter-cultural in the matter of injustice. The liturgical spirituality of the church should reveal the paschal character of the human experience of social justice. It is theologically true that every liturgy brings to expression those saving actions of Christ which we call the Paschal Mystery, namely, the death, resurrection, and ascension of Christ. But the danger is that Christ's own Passover will remain on the abstract level. Liturgy celebrates the dying and rising of Christ when it does so by means of our daily, often quite pedestrian, dyings and risings. Christians who live according to such a liturgical spirituality can be both symbol and cause of God's action in situations of injustice by embodying in their lives the justice and mercy of God. Their sacramental living, then, reveals the meaning in suffering and oppression and calls upon all persons to eliminate the demonic forces which control society.[80]

As Christ's Body, we are all deeply affected by the struggle for political, economic, and cultural freedom. In these contexts, our prophetic praxis can be understood as a means of liberation, an idea, which is very close to prophetic action. In this way we need to recognize that all our liturgical praxis must envelop a hope in which God's Word impels us to believe and to act in ways, which move humankind in the direction of a complete manifestation of the Word, which prophetically proclaims life, justice, equality, and love, and rejects all signs of death.

79. Empereur and Kiesling, *The Liturgy That Does Justice*, 253.
80. Ibid., 16–17.

The evolution of global socio-economic processes over the past decades has given rise to an astonishing and paradoxical situation. On the one hand, we can see technology reaching a high level of development and, at the same time, we can see the level of unemployment rising in both "rich" and "poor" countries, although to a much greater degree among the latter. On the other hand, the social differences between these extremes have increased to astronomic levels, augmenting even more the gap between "developed" and "under-developed" countries.

Before going any further, I must state that I would prefer not to use the terms "developed" and "under-developed" countries, or even classify them as "rich" or "poor." For me, these terms express clear evidence of a discriminatory language imposed by those benefitting from socio-economic supremacy. Certainly, none of the "under-developed" or "poor" countries would label themselves as such. They are named this way by others, not by themselves. As I see it, every single country in the world is *in the process* of finding out ways to live better and more justly, each according to its own way. In this sense, we are all "developing" countries. From the socio-economic supremacy perspective, what we have seen disguised under the auspices of freedom, quality of life, and God's blessings, is actually an ideological emphasis on socio-economic differences that serves to legitimate the *status quo*, which functions as a clear subliminal propaganda of the affluent classes in society. As a prophetic community, the church should emphasize the opposite of this subliminal propaganda, and instead draw attention to the danger of any socio-economic system that legitimates mechanisms of human exploitation and suffering in society. This socio-economic reality cannot be disregarded in any conversation concerning liturgy and social justice.

One of the key concepts in the socio-economic realm during the 1980s, and which gained usage in religious circles during the next decade, was the concept of "sustainable growth."[81] This concept, which needs to be understood not only in economic terms, but also in its social, political, cultural, and environmental dimensions, has become an indispensable tool for understanding the political-ideological tensions of our time. The term "sustainability," says Julio de Santa Ana, "basically refers to the need for human beings to recognize the limits inherent in creation and to adapt their claims on the future to a course which can be sustained—that is, maintained for an

---

81. For an extended conversation on this matter from the perspective of Christian social ethics, see Santa Ana, ed., *Sustainability and Globalization*.

indefinite time."[82] Santa Ana presents three basic elements in the definition of sustainability, which must be taken into consideration. He rightly sees sustainability as implying: (1) concern for the well-being of future generations; (2) concern for justice; and (3) concern for the threats and risks humanity is facing today.[83] A prophetic-oriented Church, concerned not only with the defense and promotion of life for future generations, but also with justice and with human safety, must not ignore the impact of these tensions in society and must find responsible ways to denounce the heavy burden these tensions may cause, especially to the life of those marginalized, or even more so, those who are among the left out, voiceless, and forgotten.

Clodovis Boff provides a significant socio-economic analysis in which the "excluded" are the central subjects. Instead of "oppressed" or "marginalized," he prefers to use "excluded" to designate those people left "to fend" for themselves; that is, to live their own destiny.[84]

Given this basic global framework, one cannot assume that this astonishing and paradoxical situation has nothing to do with liturgical practices. On the contrary, it actually challenges liturgical practices. Particularly in relation to socio-economic tensions and antagonisms, the point is to discern how liturgical experiences might be used to engage Christian communities in these crucial themes, helping them to understand the complexities, to discern ideologies, and to act responsibly, connecting faith and praxis in the spiritual and concrete world. In light of this critical situation, the Church needs to find alternative and creative answers to the question: How can our liturgy help construct a Christian socio-economic understanding in a Church that seems to be hiding itself from socio-economic concerns?

From this perspective, it can be inferred that all liturgical experiences, all human relationships, and all environmental consciousness must be rooted in a genuine gesture of love, which is the source of justice. In this sense, the primary goal of all types of Christian ministry in this globalized world is to radiate love, which is the source of inspiration for socio-economic justice.

As we saw in Chapter 1, one of the most noteworthy commitments of earlier Christian communities was to be prepared to serve the neighbor. This commitment implies a willing self-offering for the sake of the collective whole as a prompt response to God's call. It also reveals the awareness

82. Ibid., 4.
83. Ibid., 5–6.
84. See Boff, *Como Trabalhar Com Os Excluídos*.

of self-offering for the collective well-being, an engaging prophetic action, as an interconnected action between contemplative spirituality and engaged participation in the world—the "big-house" in which we live. This is possible through the liturgical theological concept of symbolic exchange by which the prophetic community of faith experiences its ultimate level of what will be explored next as *total sacramental rituality.*

4

Total Sacramental Rituality

THERE IS A CLOSE relationship between sacramental theology and anthropology, specifically with regard to anthropology's approach to ritual. The anthropological concept of ritual, presented in the work of Arnold Van Gennep,[1] has been the catalyst for my discerning a significant association between the ideas of two other authors—Louis-Marie Chauvet's sacramental concept[2] and Marcel Mauss' political-economic concept.[3] In this chapter, I connect these concepts with the liturgical theological idea of symbolic exchange by which the community of faith experiences its ultimate level of what I am calling *total sacramental rituality*. This has implications for the prophetic dimension of the liturgy. I contend that the symbolic exchange is a ritual consciousness/action by which the community of faith experiences the juxtaposition of three levels of ritual communication: The first is Chauvet's spiritual/transcendent language (theology); the second is Gennep's cultural/contextual language (culture); and the third is Mauss' socio/political/economic language (ethics). All three authors present a tripartite schema that will be used as a reference to my *total sacramental rituality* matrix. The concepts involved are: Gift—Reception—Return-Gift (Chauvet); Separation—Transition—Incorporation (Gennep); and Give—Receive—Reciprocate (Mauss).

1. Gennep, *Rites of Passage*.
2. Chauvet, *Symbol and Sacrament*.
3. Mauss, *The Gift*.

Total sacramental rituality refers to an understanding of religious praxis as active and dynamic prophetic actions in which the community of faith faces the ultimate level *in totality* of its own existence, through sacramental understanding and ritual experiences. Sacramental celebration in totality explores divine genuineness in language and rite, claims the community's identity, and promotes engaged faithful Christian life in the world. From this perspective, what is at stake is the challenge of celebrating the sacraments as a commitment to a liturgical spirituality—a prophetic action—directed to the establishment of life for all. To this end, a prophetic community of faith is called to live in spiritual unity, to praxis human reconciliation, to promote equality, and to be engaged agent of transformation.

Having this prophetic framework, the church (as celebrating community) is challenged to incorporate in its liturgical praxis the three levels of ritual communication presented above. What follows is a brief discussion of the subject of "symbolic exchange," which incorporates insights from a postmodern theological perspective. The discussion then turns to the prophetic dimension of the liturgy, the mediation of symbols, and the cultural context in which the prophetic praxis of the church takes place. Finally, the conversation will be expanded to include the three authors in this study who serve as references for the theological, cultural, and ethical foundations for the total sacramental rituality matrix.

SYMBOLIC EXCHANGE: GIFT IN ITS TOTALITY FROM POSTMODERN PERSPECTIVE

The symbolic exchange system suggested by Louis-Marie Chauvet must be examined in light of postmodern scholars who present significant philosophical and theological approaches to the concept of *gift*. Besides Chauvet and Mauss, the main resources for this task include Jacques Derrida, John Milbank, Catherine Pickstock, William Cavanaugh, and Stephen Long.

At this point, I would like to clarify my understanding of the concept postmodernity. It is essential to do so in order to make the necessary transition to a more postmodern theological approach to addressing the question of symbolic exchange system. After reading other postmodernist thinkers such as Michel Foucault, Jean-François Lyotard, Gianni Vattimo, as well as those previously discussed, I have come to the conclusion that postmodernity has no specific set of praxis and beliefs that overcome modernity. Rather, it seems that there is a postmodern attitude. This attitude is characterized by the end of universal reason, as well as the independent ego, absolute truth and any unifying (or "totalizing") metanarratives. Vattimo helps us to understand the critical overcoming of modernity's own constitutive tendencies. Vattimo affirms:

> Modernity is defined as the era of overcoming and of the new, which rapidly grows old and is immediately replaced by something still newer, in an unstoppable movement that discourages all creativity even as it demands creativity and defines the latter as the sole possible form of life . . . Since the notion of truth no longer exists, and foundation no longer functions (insofar as there is no longer a foundation for the belief in foundation, that is, in the fact that thought must 'found'), there can be no way out of modernity through a critical overcoming, for the latter is a part of modernity itself. It thus becomes clear that an alternative means must be sought, and this is the moment that could be designated as the moment of the birth of post-modernity in philosophy.[4]

A move from modern discourse that is typically postmodern is a type of hermeneutic of suspicion of any claims to "truth" or any universal claim to reason. The mark of the postmodern is the rejection of such claims, as seen in Platonic, Cartesian or Hegelian rationality.

Since all claims to truth and reason are grounded in particular social and historical situations, rendering them relative to one another, the search for "truth" has, for the postmodernist, become just another power game. However, the postmodern critique does have things to teach us, and ignoring it would not be beneficial. It has something to say to Christian discourse as well, especially in the radical criticism of philosophers like Foucault, Derrida, and Lyotard. Postmodern philosophers' critique of modernity and humanism, along with their proclamation of the death of "man" and development of new perspectives on society, on knowledge, on discourse, on historicity, and on power, have made these thinkers a major influence on postmodern thought. They draw upon an anti-Enlightenment tradition that rejects the equation of reason, emancipation, and progress, arguing that an interface between modern forms of power and knowledge has served to create new forms of domination. The end of modernity, which in Milbank's words means "the end of a single system of truth based on universal reason," is not yet accomplished.[5] In this in-between process

4. Vattimo, *The End of Modernity*, 166–67.
5. Ward, ed., *The Postmodern God*, 265.

of modernity twilight and postmodernity dawn, one can only speculate theological concepts and risk philosophical lucubration about their implications for living Christian *praxis*. In a postmodern perspective, the social-political-economic-religious narratives need to be deconstructed and subverted with suspicion as universal truth in order to overcome nihilistic assumptions.[6] In sum, it is this postmodern philosophical theological ground which I have been challenged to walk through.

At this point some necessary questions must be raised. In what way does postmodernity configure the symbolic exchange system suggested by Chauvet? That is to say, how is the theological concept of *gift* shaped by postmodernity? What do postmodern scholars have to say about the immanent exchange of a transcendental gift?

In Milbank's writing, we encounter the question, "Can a gift be given?"[7] In his essay, which carries that very same question as its title, Milbank suggests that "*agape* is the consummation of gift-exchange,"[8] in which two features can really be distinguished: (1) there must be delay of return; and (2) the gift given back must be different. In this sense, he asserts that if a gift can be given at all, it must be within the *logos* or measure of a necessary *delay* and there must be *non-identical repetition* between gift and counter-gift. For Milbank, it is suspicious to repeat and to immediately reciprocate gifts. Therefore he calls our attention to the saying, "On the contrary, it is to repeat differently, in order to repeat, exactly, the content of Christ's life, and to wait, by a necessary delay, the answering repetition of the other that will fold temporal linearity back into the eternal circle of the triune life."[9] Accordingly, a gift is characterized as gift only through the new covenant that sustains a "prophetic delay" and "non-identical repetition:"

6. Here I follow Vattimo's understanding and use of Nietzsche's theory of *nihilism* as the radical repudiation of value, meaning and desirability. See Vattimo, *The End of Modernity*.

7. Milbank, "Can a Gift be Given? Prolegomena to a Future Trinitarian Metaphysic," 119–61.

8. Ibid., 144. Dussel also relates *agape* with gift. But Dussel does not suggests recompense or return that may come as response to gestures of love, *agape*. He says. "For Jesus, . . . real love is *agape* . . . It is love for the other in view of that other's own reality, though I myself may receive nothing from that other . . . It is 'gift' (the denotation of *charis* in the Greek of the New Testament, from Luke 1:30 to John 1:14); the gift of oneself, commitment, surrender, self-donation without recompense: 'There is no greater love than this: to lay down one's life for one's friend' (John 15:13)" (see Dussel, *Ethics and Community*, 10).

9. Milbank, "Can a Gift be Given?," 150.

99

agape. Since *agape* is the consummation of gift-exchange, Milbank claims it to be not as "pure gift," as it is claimed to be in archaic milieu (Mauss), but as "purified gift-exchange," which remains "within the bounds of the ontological, which is to say the metaphysical."[10] With regard to the theme of *delay*, it seems that Catherine Pickstock has a different approach. She says: "[O]ne can speak of a "return" indissociable from the act of giving, simultaneous with it, a condition of its possibility, and yet not reducible to an economic market exchange—not reducible because the return is not simply something one is hoping to receive later, but is something one is already receiving in giving."[11] In regard to the theme of *giving, gift, and return*, Pickstock offers an important approach to be considered. She argues that the act of giving holds in itself the immediate return. For her, the return gift is not something one is expecting to receive later, but is a reality one is already receiving in giving. In Pickstock's account, the two movements of "receiving" and "passing on" are mutually constitutive, in which the act of receiving is "indistinguishable from" the counter-gift of return. Pickstock goes even further, saying, "receiving is itself returning."[12] For her, this is a complex system, which reveals the ambiguity of the "gift-relation" between the worshipper and God. In affirming the mutuality of returning (transmitting) gift, she states:

> For this is not a matter of subsequent stages of "responses" whereby we first receive our true humanity from Christ, and then receive the gift of divinity and the gift of being able to offer. In reality, this is all one gift, forever repeated differently, whose lineaments cannot be disentangled without seeming to be laid out in stages: we receive our capacity to receive in receiving that which we are to receive; to receive our humanity, we must already receive the gratuitous excess of divinity, and to receive the gift of humanity and divinity, we must already have begun to transmit this gift.[13]

Pickstock also claims that there can be no "return" for the transcendent gift. Yet, she affirms that it can only be returned with *difference*. She says, "Our return is to receive again, differently . . . The 'return' is to receive and repeat. We go on calling upon God, even when He is within us. We cannot exhaust

---

10. Ibid., 131.
11. Pickstock, *After Writing*, 112.
12. Ibid.
13. Ibid., 242.

Him, but offer a 'return' by receiving Him again and again."[14] For me, this is not a transcendental commodity precisely because there is no equivalence where one transcendental "value" equals another human return "value." In this sense, I can agree with Pickstock when she says that transcendental gift can only be returned with *difference*. It does not represent, by any means, a type of contract in inter-human exchange, which, according to Stephen Long, would be inconsistent with Christian virtue.

Long helps us to understand the difference between contracts and gifts. He writes: "Contracts assume disinterested exchanges based on two individuals' sacrifice and alienation of their commodities. Gifts, on the other hand, assume that what we give—our daily labor, our professional activities, our time and energy—cannot be thoroughly sacrificed and alienated from us, but in fact extend our being as participants in the lives of those who receive them."[15] This is a necessary distinction precisely because transcendental gift, by nature, is inexhaustible and, unlike contracts, can only be returned with *difference*. It must be returned in the economy of love, which bears no obligation. In Pickstock's account, this is a complex system. It reveals the ambiguity of the "gift-relation" between the worshipper and God.

In his essay "Postmodern Critical Augustinianism," Milbank presents the idea of "sacrifice-offering," a self-giving act. Thus, "in Christianity, God is thought of as asking only for the offering of our free will, in a return of love to him. This is no longer in any sense a self-destruction or self-division, but rather a self-fulfillment, an offering that is at the same time our reception of the fullness of Being."[16] This is to say, an offering of ourselves in love as a response to God's self-giving act in the flesh is exchanged in Eucharistic celebration, where the community of faith experiences the fullness of Being, God's gift, God's action, and God's initiative, which in turn requires response.

Milbank's book *The Word Made Strange: Theology, Language, Culture* presents a passionate philosophical and theological dialogue between recent thinkers, with special reference to Jean-Luc Marion. In this work, Milbank exchanges philosophical ideas with Heidegger, Husserl, Levinas, Nietzsche, and Descartes, to name just a few. He cites Marion as a philosopher of transcendental phenomenology who discards the theological correlation

14. Ibid., 247.

15. Long, *Divine Economy*, 268.

16. Milbank, "Postmodern Critical Augustinianism," 265–78, 271.

with philosophy concerning "Being," in favor of a correlation concerning "donation" or "gift." With regard to these assumptions, we can ask: What is a gift? What is that "gift" which is given before, beyond and without Being, a donation we cannot even name—Being / Nothing? Is this "gift" a projection of ourselves? If so, is it simply a reduction of God as a mirror of our existential ego? How can theological terms such as "grace," "sacrifice," Christ's "paschal mystery," and "presence" be conceived in Marion's transcendental phenomenology in relation to Heidegger's onto-theology philosophy?

In order to answer these questions, Milbank, interpreting Marion's work, suggests that "while we must receive, or give back through gratitude the gift, for it to be there for us, this giving back is, nonetheless, a pre-ontological precondition for our very subjective existence."[17] It is in terms of "Being" as plenitude and transcendental, that one should understand theological terms such as those presented above. They are not compatible with a temporal "present" as suspicious appropriation. Rather, we must see them as incorporated into the sacramental transcendental gift, the fullness of Being: God's gift which is given, appropriated, and reciprocated.

William Cavanaugh is also influenced by Jean-Luc Marion's work, especially *God Without Being*. He shows appreciation for Marion's treatment of the issue of "presence." Cavanaugh sees the latter as gift. He emphasizes Marion's defense of transubstantiation based on seeing the Eucharistic presence as gift (*corpus mysticum*). Cavanaugh agrees that Christ's presence in the Eucharist is not temporal, that is, not in the here and now, not in ordinary time. Rather, it is "the present, meaning 'gift,' of Christ's self in a way that encompasses the whole Christ: past, future, and present."[18] In this sense a preferable term would be "Eucharistic presence" rather than "real presence."

Pickstock's first approach to this particular theological issue is presented as a dialogue with Derrida's text *The Gift of Death*.[19] For Derrida, death is the only possibility of "pure gift." This is precisely because of the supremely unreturnable characteristic of death, assuming that one's death is *one's own*. Derrida's claim for ethical responsibility is based on "the possibility of dying *of* the other or *for* the other."[20] He suggests this ethical responsibility

17. Milbank, *The Word Made Strange*, 42—43.

18. Cavanaugh, *Torture and Eucharist*, 227.

19. Originally published as "Donner la Mort," in Rabaté and Wetzel, eds., *L'éthique Du Don*.

20. Derrida, *The Gift of Death*, 48.

is instituted "as a *putting-oneself-to-death* or *offering-one's-death*, that is, giving one's life, in the ethical dimension of sacrifice."[21] Pickstock points to the same idea. She suggests that a theological alternative "would be to assume that *nothing* is one's, but rather that everything, life and death alike, arrive not as possessions but as gifts."[22] As I understand it, this is actually a political enterprise, one which challenges all of us to pass on what we have already received, God's gift of unconditional grace, which we receive thoroughly, in totality, in the sacraments.

As a final observation, one may ask a simple question: What is at stake in a postmodern theological construct? Actually, in a postmodern sense, there is no specific answer for this type of question. I sympathize with A.K.M. Adam's statement that, "Even if postmodernity is not any one thing, it is some things more than others."[23] Therefore, any attempt to answer such a question will be vulnerable to postmodern criticism. Nonetheless, since there is no way to escape, I would risk suggesting that, from the perspective of total sacramental rituality, we must celebrate symbolic exchange with *difference*, which leads to transformation: gift for the life of the world. From this perspective, it is possible to say that the sacramental life of the church has the potential of transforming old oppressive realities into new redemptive experiences of liberation with *difference*. It is a transposition from an old state without God's presence (total gift) into a new state infused with God's mercy: God's self-giving. As Crockett suggests, "When the meal is celebrated in thanksgiving for the gifts of creation, the community that celebrates it cannot fail to seek justice for all God's creation."[24] A prophetic community is called to act with commitment against so many other factors that compromise the dignity of human beings and the stability of the created order. As will be described later in this chapter, it is by celebrating total sacramental rituality that symbolic exchange has the most fundamental expression of transformation. The prophetic community is a transforming community—transforming and always being transformed as a visible sign of symbolic exchange. Sacrament is one of the core places where the prophetic dimension can and should be encountered.

---

21. Ibid.

22. Pickstock, *After Writing*, 111–12.

23. Adam, *What Is Postmodern Biblical Criticism?*, 1.

24. Crockett, *Eucharist: Symbol of Transformation*, 262.

THE PROPHETIC DIMENSION OF THE SACRAMENT

The concept of sacrament was discussed at length in chapter two. Nonetheless, I want now to consider its relevance for a prophetic consciousness. As Christians, we can ask: How can we live prophetically the sacramentality of Christian existence in a world that seems to be far from spiritual and communal consciousness?

Sacramentality, I would say, is the nest of theology—an invisible place where foundational symbolic understanding gives birth to beliefs that grow in visible praxis. In other words, sacramentality is one of the constitutive dimensions of faith by which grace—the "non-value" gift—is fully given and nurtured by praxis. A prophetic sacramentality calls for a response, a return, and an exchange. As any other exchanging action, it depends on the mediation of symbols.

Symbols are important in the sacramental realm precisely because they constitute the vehicle, the mediation of grace or "symbolic exchange," by which Christian identity finds its concrete completion. The symbolic emerges when things participate in a ritual action and people who participate in it hear their narratives, understand their meanings, and claim them as their own. A thing becomes a symbol when we appropriate the significance of its mystery.

Thus, in the sacramental context, symbols are effective media that legitimate beliefs and behaviors. They are not merely static signs. Symbols effectively participate in sacramental actions. For José Severino Croatto, there is no religious experience without symbol. He says, "Every religious expression is symbolic, and it is not experienced without symbol: a fact that opens roads and guides."[25] Symbol is a necessary component of religious language precisely because, as Croatto points out, symbol is polysemic (or "pluri-valent," another term in Croatto's language), relational, permanent, universal, pre-hermeneutic, and totalizing.[26]

Clifford Geertz and Victor Turner offer important insights that help us understand and incorporate in life the meaning, effect, and affect of the

---

25. Croatto, *Los Lenguajes de la Experiencia Religiosa: Estudio De Fenomenologia De La Religión* [The Languages of Religious Experience: Study on Religion Phenomenology], 16. Maldonado, in his book *El sentido litúrgico* [*The Liturgical Sense*], says "there cannot be experience of God and access to God without symbols." See Maldonado, *El Sentido Litúrgico*, 130; translation mine.

26. For a descriptive approach to these concepts, see Croatto, *Los Lenguajes De La Experiencia Religiosa*, 75–82.

realm of symbols in human existence. They offer an ethnographic approach, an interpretation, and a contextual analysis to the subject. Both bring the consistent and recurring understanding that symbols are fundamental ingredients for supporting social-cultural-religious values. As Turner says, "symbols are essentially involved in social process."[27] For this reason, I would emphasize that we need to incorporate, in sacramental practices, those values that challenge the social-cultural-religious status quo and seek transformation.

As stated before, the symbolic emerges when things, objects, or entities, tell their narratives and we hear them through ritual actions. Symbols have meaning, symbolic meaning, that points to a different reality or realities. For Turner, the meaning of a symbol "derives from its relationship to other symbols in a totality, a Gestalt, whose elements acquire their significance from the system as a whole."[28] That is why, in phenomenology of religion, symbols are conceived as having polysemic, multiple meanings.

Geertz states, "It is a cluster of sacred symbols, woven into some sort of ordered whole, which makes up a religious system."[29] In this sense, it is possible to affirm that, in the realm of religion, symbols or "symbol complexes," are cultural values in which a particular social structure legitimates its religious reality. As such, symbols interact and communicate messages that can be read in cultural and religious contexts. As Ione Buyst puts it, "Symbols are not things, but rather relations. They depend on a communication process."[30] Therefore, in a liturgical milieu, symbols are dependent upon different levels of language interactions in both cultural and ritual contexts. In sacramental understanding, they are a powerful, transformative mediation that consists of more than the mere elements of water, bread, and wine. They actually embody and put into effect the promises they claim to bring about, as they ritually communicate and interact with the larger cultural context of which the faith community is a part. By experiencing the sacramental symbolic message, through ritual and culture, the whole celebrating community is spiritually nurtured and prepared to live out its faith and to act as a means of grace and transformation.

27. Turner, *The Forest of Symbols*, 20.

28. Ibid., 51.

29. Geertz, *The Interpretation of Cultures*, 129.

30. Buyst, *Los Símbolos En La Liturgia* [*The Symbols in the Liturgy*], 7; translation mine. The original is in Portuguese: *Símbolos na Liturgia*.

Cultural sensitivity has in itself the potential for transformation. The cultural implication for the prophetic dimension of the sacrament must not be left behind. Some questions, then, help to fuel the passion for this investigation: What role does culture play in the sacramental life of the church? How can members of the Church conceive, process, and assimilate their own culture through language, rituals, and symbolic patterns seen and experienced in their everyday life? Are there substantial elements in culture that can give reference to the celebrating community, inciting them to act as agents of social-political-economic transformation?

These questions lead us to the core issue to which anthropologists and theologians have made indispensable contributions in the field of cross-cultural studies: the interplay between culture and religious practice. On the one hand, anthropologists grant us a very broad sense and understanding of culture as the totality of the social environment and the central interaction into which a human being is born and in which he or she constructs and develops social and religious behaviors. On the other hand, Christian theologians grant us religious principles, which govern, or should govern, the behavior of a Christian, as well as inform their application to different social circumstances. The character and interpretation of these religious practices have been the subject of a rich theological debate that has spanned the whole of human history down to our own time. Their sources are scripture, reason inspired by faith and life, and the teaching of the church.

The downside on the part of sociologists and cultural anthropologists in this attempt to approach the dialogue between culture and the sacramental community is that, most of the time, these scholars use specific language to describe research in a way that most lay and non-theologically trained people in the church cannot understand and assimilate. The problem here is not the church member's lack of knowledge in the social science field; rather, it is that the majority of social science scholars do not address the content of the field in direct connection with the life of the church. Sociologists and anthropologists, in general, are not concerned with making social, religious, and cultural issues understandable to the worshipping community. The question, then, is how the celebrating community can be able to understand its own *sitz im leben* in order to recognize dialectically the signs of good and evil, life and death. In doing so, the celebrating community can act critically and prophetically, renewing itself while seeking transformation. In other words, the whole process of celebrating together should facilitate the community's awareness of the Christian historical trajectory, a consciousness of its cultural unity, and attentiveness to the transformative resonance of Christian liturgical practices in the world.

As noted previously, the social sciences, especially sociology and anthropology, provide excellent instruments of social analysis. These critical and analytical tools are not beyond the reach of the church. With the utilization of the social sciences, along with responsible theological discernment, it is possible to envision new liturgical practices where the "common Christian tradition" (that which is essential in Christian liturgical practices throughout Christian history) is retained and the new is welcomed in order to create a liturgy, which legitimates and eternalizes the community's spiritual experiences toward transformation. This expression is used not only in relation to what exists in common in a denominational sense, but is also to be understood in relation to what exists in even the most remote Christian liturgical practice. This historical identity is related to the imperishable reality of the liturgical Christian tradition. A responsibly prophetic vision provides the new and transitory without renouncing the historically permanent. This posture is based on the need to preserve what was and still is significant for the sake of Christian identity. The liturgical celebration represents the very core of this identity. There are many expressive liturgical symbols, gestures, acts, words, and texts that must be saved from being forgotten, and thus lost. It is not unusual to observe the tendency today, in many Christian circles, to refuse some liturgical acts just because they seem to belong to other Christian tradition. Unfortunately, these Christian segments have undervalued the Christian historic trajectory of these practices. How can people understand the tremendous symbolic value of liturgical treasures that have endured for generations? How can these symbolic treasures be available to future generations if we fail to keep them alive in our regular celebrations? How can we be a prophetic community without reaffirming consciously the past, living critically the present, and envisioning creatively the future? We must look in as many different directions as possible.

Tradition has to do with memory. There is a Jewish proverb that says, "Memory is the pillar of redemption and forgetfulness is the beginning of death."[31] The common Christian tradition has in its foundation the concept

31. I was first introduced to this Jewish dictum in 1983. It was assigned as reference for the final paper of the "History of the Jewish Thought" class, during my Bachelor in Theology in the Methodist Seminary in São Paulo—Brazil. The assignment was given without direct quotation to its bibliographical source. Recently, I found one citation in

of memory. Religious practice without memory is condemned to death. Tradition and memory in liturgical contexts are directly related to historical identity. They are related to the imperishable reality of the liturgical Christian tradition. For some people, to say yes to tradition seems too archaic, reactionary, or means retreating to the past. Opposition to this perspective is a central concern of this book. That is to say, a major barrier to understanding the sacrament as prophetic voice is forgetfulness. Christianity, in its essence, is about memory.

This principle of continuity of the common Christian tradition is based on helping to keep alive what was, is, and will be significant to our core Christian identity. The sacraments represent the very center of our practice of remembrance/memory—*anamnesis*. This vision provides room for the new and transitory without renouncing the historically permanent. We need to value tradition critically and responsibly in order to learn from the Church's mistakes as well as from its most expressive and authentic teachings.

Kathryn Tanner is helpful in clarifying the role of tradition in supporting Christian identity. She asserts that, "Christian identity is sustained across differences of time and place if Christian cultural materials retain their identity when transmitted from one time and place to another and/or if the processes that transmit them do. Tradition refers here both to what is transmitted—the cultural materials—and to the processes by which they are transmitted."[32] This perspective helps us to understand how Christianity and culture are tied together, and how a Christian community has a responsible role in preserving its own cultural identity.

Sacrament is essentially a religious memorial act, *anamnesis*. Without memory there is no eschatological hope. As was mentioned before, Rubem Alves emphasizes the memorial character of the sacrament when he says that sacraments make us think about return. "Think about return" brings remembrance—*anamnesis*. It is an act of thinking about the past, yet living in the present and envisioning the future. This is not a static action. It has a sense of active continuity and eschatological expectation of what is to come—the promise of a new heaven and a new earth, where justice, love, and peace flow like streams of water, *maranatha*. Because Jesus came into the world (*epiphany*), as the incarnated Gift from God, he offered himself

---

English with no reference to the sources: Hauerwas and Wells, eds., *The Blackwell Companion to Christian Ethics*, 397.

32. Tanner, *Theories of Culture*, 128–29.

as a visible gift to everyone who celebrates his memorial sacrifice. This is a visible sign, and an anticipation of the fellowship we will celebrate in the coming time (*eschatology*), where there will be places for many, not just for some. The meal in which Christ is remembered announces and establishes the presence of God's kingdom just as it was shared with all during Christ's ministry in our midst.

William Crockett also helps us to understand the sacramental and redemptive meaning we celebrate in the Eucharistic memorial. He says, "Through the Eucharistic memorial, the sacrifice of the cross is made sacramentally present in order that we may participate in its redemptive reality in the present."[33] The memorial (*anamnesis*) of Christ's life, death, and resurrection (paschal mystery) must be spread beyond the limits of the local community. This memorial character of the sacramental celebration is the theological foundation for prophetic practice. The prophetic dimension of the sacramental practice of the Church dwells in the ability to see and interpret Christ's paschal mystery and spread it with courage in order to transform the world for the sake of the humanity.

LEVELS OF RITUAL LANGUAGE: THEOLOGY, CULTURE, AND ETHICS

Every time an individual or a community celebrates the birth of a baby, the happiness of graduation, the engagement of religious practice, the harvesting of a fruitful season, the return from war, or the overcoming of anti-life situations, it is a time for ritual performances. But I have to admit that this affirmation is not a reality everywhere. At least, in my Brazilian Protestant religious heritage, to call upon "ritual" for religious celebration is an inaccurate statement, for it could be mistakenly connected to mystic or magic practices. Apart from the ordinary Sunday services, prayer services and Bible studies, and other special services such as funerals, marriages, baptisms, ordination, consecration, and the Eucharist, the community could not experience any other type of religious practice, and worse, it could not even think of them as rituals. Regrettably, a few decades ago, the term "ritual" was not even part of the vocabulary of some Brazilian Protestant groups.

Tom Driver, while discussing his religious heritage, seems to have had the same experience, i.e., the word ritual was kept distant from his religious practice. He says, "We had 'worship services,' or 'church services,'

33. Crockett, *Eucharist, Symbol of Transformation*, 231.

or just 'plain church,' but not 'rituals.'"[34] Driver continues, "In our language 'church service' referred to something God-given and true, while 'ritual' was viewed with suspicion as some kind of esoteric activity practiced by people of 'other faiths.'"[35] This is particularly remarkable because it emphasizes how far we were from perceiving ritual as part of our life. Again Driver helps us to understand that "rituals belong to us, and we to them, as surely as do our language and culture. The human choice is not *whether* to ritualize but when, how, where, and why."[36] Sometimes we miss opportunities to experience signs of life in our family or in our community of faith just because we do not ritualize.

Rituals have the power of transformation. Transformation happens when, through ritual understanding and practice, the community appropriates what Linda Vogel suggests: "Name your joys and your pains. Claim and tell and retell your stories. Find connections with your stories and the stories of your faith community. Create liturgies or rituals that can help you, and those who share life's faith journey with you, to focus on who and Whose you are and what it means to be experiencing losses or new beginnings."[37] The desire for change legitimates rituals. Rituals are born when desire is present. When individuals, families, and congregations are not experiencing the inner desire for telling and retelling who and Whose they are, rituals will not be signs of new beginning.

As Herbert Anderson and Edward Foley have suggested, "rituals not only construct reality and make meaning . . . rituals are essential and powerful means for making the world a habitable and hospitable place."[38] The desire for change makes ritual efficacious. Desire overcomes fear and makes change possible. Ritual is the visible sign, the seal, and the ground for transformative practices.

From his reading of Bruce Kapferer's phenomenological approach to ritual study,[39] Anderson suggests three modes of ritual practices: "1) Ritual performance is a communicative event that discloses, or perhaps manifests, a particular complex of meanings and relationships. 2) Ritual performance is experienced in the present and as such has a "prereflective" meaning.

34. Driver, *Liberating Rites*, 6.
35. Ibid., 6–7.
36. Ibid., 6.
37. Vogel, *Rituals for Resurrection*, 103–4.
38. Anderson and Foley, *Mighty Stories, Dangerous Rituals*, 20, 22.
39. Kapferer, *A Celebration of Demons*.

3) Ritual performance offers the possibility for the transformation or construction of meaning, relationships, and ways of being."[40] Anderson's third model of ritual performance is of particular interest in the theological, cultural, and ethical levels of ritual languages that are developed in the sequence.

CONTRIBUTION OF LOUIS-MARIE CHAUVET

Louis-Marie Chauvet, in his book *Symbol and Sacrament*, suggests that only through "symbolic exchange" can we think theologically about the sacramentality of the church. Symbolic exchange happens when the community experiences the spiritual/transcendent-language level of ritual communication. In this level of ritual communication, the community: (1) partakes of the Logos, which is the sacramentality of faith/identity (gift); (2) stands as recipient of God's self-giving through sacramental practice (reception); and (3) nurtures its spirituality in being the true Body of Christ in the world (return-gift).[41] To access faith requires acceptance that (1) the Scriptures are a living Word of God for us today; (2) the liturgical and sacramental celebration reclaims the memory of the life, death, and resurrection of the Son of God (paschal mystery); and (3) the human ethic, personal or communal, must be a response to God's love through Jesus Christ, serving each other without prejudice.

The representation Chauvet uses to illustrate what I am calling the "spiritual/transcendent-language" level of ritual communication is the "symbolic exchange" structure (Gift—Reception—Return-Gift). It is built on three principles, which sustain the Christian identity and in which the Christian faith finds its constitutive dimension: Scripture, sacraments, and ethics. This structure is well-fitted, by definition, as "a whole formed of co-ordinated phenomena, such that each depends on the others and could not be what it is without its relation to them."[42] Chauvet presents a diagram,[43] as shown below, which represents the process of symbolic exchange as follows: *Gift—Reception—Return-Gift.*

---

40. Anderson, *Practicing Ourselves*, 93.
41. Chauvet, *Symbol and Sacrament*, 278–80.
42. Ibid., 161.
43. Ibid., 278.

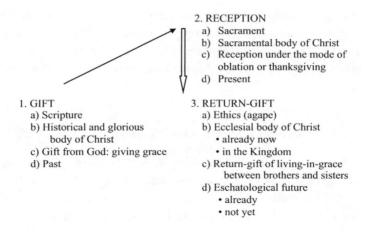

2. RECEPTION
a) Sacrament
b) Sacramental body of Christ
c) Reception under the mode of oblation or thanksgiving
d) Present

1. GIFT
a) Scripture
b) Historical and glorious body of Christ
c) Gift from God: giving grace
d) Past

3. RETURN-GIFT
a) Ethics (agape)
b) Ecclesial body of Christ
 • already now
 • in the Kingdom
c) Return-gift of living-in-grace between brothers and sisters
d) Eschatological future
 • already
 • not yet

A question comes to mind at this point, namely: What makes this diagram of *symbolic exchange* a paradigm for Christian sacramental understanding? The response is unequivocal: Christ himself as the Gift from God. Chauvet argues:

> To see this Christian uniqueness in our diagram of the process of identity, we must remind ourselves that the 'object' placed into circulation in the exchange is Christ himself and that he comes to us in his threefold body through the Spirit: he is the gratuitous gift announced in the Scripture; he is the object sacramentally received in the Church's 'giving thanks;' he is the object entrusted to the ethical responsibility of believers—by the 'spiritual sacrifice' (anti-sacrifice) of their agape, he raises up a body for himself within humanity.[44]

The position of "gift" is specified as "Scripture" which is the obligatory point of departure. It points to theological demands where the Scripture is recognized as a gift from God. In my estimation, it also points to prophetic liturgical celebrations where the community of faith receives God's word and proclaims the truth of love, justice, and equality.

In the first leg of the Christian identity structure presented by Chauvet, Scripture has a place of central importance regarding the Christian faith. For it is exactly from Scripture that believers can find their identity through the memorial character of a confession of faith performed liturgically. Thus, the celebrating community partakes of the Scripture in order to legitimate and to revitalize its faith. The social-historical-cultural character

---

44. Ibid., 289.

of Scripture plays an inevitable role in the community's faith and in framing its sacramental identity. The opposite operates with the same level of importance; that is, the celebrating practice of the Christian community launches epistemologically the character of the Scripture.

From my perspective, the community is nurtured by the proclamation of the Word, by the revelation of God. The proclamation is inserted in several moments of worship. It happens through reading the Word, through prayer, visual resources, singing, liturgical texts, through dramas, and most obviously, through the homily (preaching). As the Word is proclaimed in these different moments, the community solidifies its faith, grows in hope, nourishes on the truth, promotes guidance for its members, and remains determined in the central message of the Gospel: justice, peace and equality among peoples. The proclamation of the Word, then, confirms the prophetic character of the community as a source of spiritual nourishment and energy to fulfilling the mission.

The position of "reception" is specified as "Sacrament" and defined as a point of passage. It points to living sacramental celebrations where the community of faith receives Christ's sacramental gifts and gives thanks. In my understanding, it also points to the prophetic commitment of partaking water, bread, and the cup, which are Christ's sacramental symbols of transformation and abundant life for all.

The second leg of the Christian identity structure is the sacramental life of the church. The Christian community will grow in faith when the whole meaning of the sacramental celebration is not conceived, according to Chauvet's arguments, as "joined to a scheme of cause-and-effect and to a representation of the sacraments as channels or, even more, as containers of grace or else as instruments for the injection of a germ."[45] Rather it will grow through repeating the gestures, words, and life of the Risen One in memory of him for the sake of the whole creation. Chauvet goes beyond saying that there is no "possible access to faith, . . . without what will later be called the *sacraments* of the Church."[46] Through the sacraments, the Church nurtures itself with God's gifts in order to be a means of grace and a sign of transformation in the world.

The position of "return-gift" is specified as "Ethics," which is defined as a point of arrival. It points to the agape, living-in-grace, between brothers and sisters, where the Spirit strengthens the community to make practical

45. Ibid., 175.
46. Ibid., 163.

ethics possible. For me, it points to prophetic actions, where brothers and sisters, inspired by the power of the Holy Spirit, act in justice and mercy as an expression of return-gift to God.

The third leg of the Christian identity structure is ethical praxis. This is the place of Christian mission where faith will be expressed in a "life of witness" defined as the ethical witness, the ethical praxis. It is in enacting God's love—that is also to say, in mission—where Christians express the ultimate meaning of the sacramentality of faith. This is why Chauvet declares firmly that, "the liturgical and sacramental expressions of the faith are constitutive dimensions of evangelization itself. Hence the contemporary insistence on a catechetical program that is 'sacramentally structured.'"[47] In another place he argues, "and the sacred work, the cult, the sacrifice that is pleasing to God, is the confession of faith lived in the agape of sharing in service to the poorest, of reconciliation, and of mercy"[48] which is a concrete and authentic work of the Spirit as "liturgy of the neighbor."[49]

Chauvet concentrates his efforts on demonstrating the dimension of *the sacramentality of the faith* as a model of the Christian identity structure. This threefold structure is well—defined as interconnected phenomena where each part depends on the others and could not be what it is without the others. The principle ruling the symbolic exchange is one of abundant graciousness. There are connections, alliances, recognitions, and remembrances; in sum, there is identification between giver and receiver. Theologically it is possible to say that there is *grace*, which is God's gift. The theological significance of *Gift* is that it functions outside of the order of value. *Gifts* exchanged in the realm of the symbolic have the phenomenological particularity of non-value. They participate in the "symbolic exchange" structure, and represent a fundamental part of our Christian identity. He says, "The good health of the faith requires that it rest on the *tripod* of Christian identity; to attempt to stand on only one or two of these legs means that we risk tipping over."[50] The "symbolic exchange" structure has as its principle a theological dimension that can be expressed as gift—reception—return-gift, through which, as I see it, the Triune God manifests God's self to humankind in totality: Creator-Redeemer-Comforter. The sacraments are the theological places for the manifestation of the Triune

47. Ibid., 221.
48. Ibid., 260.
49. Ibid., 265.
50. Ibid., 176.

divine in its fullness. The challenge for Christian communities is not only to understand theologically the mediation of the water, bread, and wine as God's gift, but also to incorporate the graciousness of the "symbolic exchange" system that challenges us, as the Body of Christ, to the return-gift, through the Spirit, in prophetic actions that transform the world. It is remarkable that Chauvet relates all these principles in a structure for Christian faith in which each part of the tripod of Christian identity is indispensable. His "symbolic exchange" plays an important role as a *theological* reference for the matrix of *total sacramental rituality*.

CONTRIBUTION OF ARNOLD VAN GENNEP

In *The Rites of Passage*, van Gennep identifies key moments of life changes and describes them as ceremonies of passage that mark a transitional social position in a given cultural context. In essence, rites of passage are transformative. These life changes include birth, puberty, initiation into social and familial groups, marriage, pregnancy, childbirth, and death.[51] In most cultural contexts, these rituals stand as keys to determining the community's social relationships and structures of power.

One of van Gennep's descriptions of society is his metaphorical understanding of it as "a house divided into rooms and corridors."[52] For him, the more complex the society, "the thinner are its internal partitions, and the wider and more open are its doors of communication. In a semicivilized [sic] society, on the other hand, sections are carefully isolated, and passage

51. In Gennep's account, rites of passage could be summarized as rites which accompany every change of place, state, social position and age. The *Encyclopedia of Religion*, ed. Eliade, defines rites of passage in the following way: "Rites of passage are a category of rituals that mark the passage of a person through the life cycle, from one stage to another over time, from one role or social position to another, integrating the human and cultural experiences with biological destiny: birth, reproduction, and death. These ceremonies make the basic distinctions, observed in all groups, between young and old, male and female, living and dead. The interplay of biology and culture is at the heart of all rites of passage, and the struggle between these two spheres asserts the essential paradox of our mortal heritage. As humans, we dwell in an equivocal world, for we belong to both nature and culture, as Claude Lévi-Strauss has pointed out. It is through rites of passage that we are able to contemplate, to formulate and reformulate, our ambivalent condition of animal and human. Biology dictates the fundamentals of our experience—birth, reproduction, and death—yet the ways in which we manipulate and modify these imperatives through cultural means are endless" (see Eliade and Adams, *The Encyclopedia of Religion*, 12:380).

52. Gennep, *Rites of Passage*, 26.

from one to another must be made through formalities and ceremonies."[53] In van Gennep's analysis, the heart of the matter is corporate participation in the human process of change and transformation. Complex societies isolate individuals, and less complex societies (semi-civilized societies, in van Gennep's language) approximate them. Is this a possible explanation for why our churches tend to deviate from ritual practices because of the churches' complexity? Following van Gennep's assumption, one can observe that the levels of communication in the church are so wide and the church is so partitioned in itself that ritual languages are not assimilated and understood in the fullness of their meaning and even less, the relevance of their existence is not valorized.

In the present cultural world, less complex societies are a rare cultural occurrence. In my understanding, this is the main contribution van Gennep offers to those concerned with transformation in society. We must value the significance of ritual practices and their ability to bring together communal cultural interests for the sake of the collectivity. Through rituals, changes can happen.

Since van Gennep's contributions come from the anthropological approach to ritual, I want to connect the discussion by linking it to theology. This will bring the two into dialog. From an anthropological perspective, one can acknowledge that theology cannot be separated from culture; and from a theological perspective, it would raise suspicion to assume that there is anthropology apart from religious experience.[54] Theologians, as well as anthropologists, are human beings engaged in religious-cultural contexts. They are influenced by, and yet they have the ability to influence, other human beings. The results of both anthropologists' and theologians' works are mutually influential. They will affect human behavior within a particular cultural focus, which in turn will inevitably affect religious contexts. Thus, the theological and anthropological interpretative task, in search of meaning, is essentially an analytical and dialogical one, which connects human beings' historic trajectory in a given culture and religious practice. Theology and anthropology need to dialogue with each other in seeking alternatives for better human life, which is the subject of both fields. The

53. Ibid.

54. For an approach to an ongoing dialogue between anthropology and theology, see Adams and Salamone, *Anthropology and Theology*; Comblin, *Retrieving the Human*; Pannenberg, *Anthropology in Theological Perspective*; and Schnelle, *The Human Condition*.

achievements of both fields impact the social, the political, and the cultural contexts in society.

Abraham Joshua Heschel provides an example when he inquires as to the standards by which we measure culture. He continues, saying: "It is customary to evaluate a nation by the magnitude of its scientific contributions or the quality of its artistic achievements. However, the true standard by which to gauge a culture is the extent to which reverence, compassion, justice are to be found in the daily lives of a whole people, not only in the acts of isolated individuals. Culture is a style of living compatible with the grandeur of being human."[55] Heschel's stance has both theological and anthropological implications in the sense that it encompasses meanings, values, and ethical elements present in human relationships. In my perspective, the dialogue between anthropology and theology happens in the ambit of culture. At the intersection of these two axes stands the cultural identity of the community. Certainly this dialogue grants that theology and what theologians do is important to what anthropology is and what anthropologists do. Therefore, it is inevitable to assume that anthropologists deal with the beliefs and religious practices of others. On the other hand, this interdisciplinary approach provides to theologians significant, consistent, and accurate theological formulations grounded on human experiences. While respecting the distinctiveness of the other, theologians need to read anthropology as much as anthropologists need to read theology.

Ritual is one of the foundational grounds where the dialogue between theology and anthropology takes place in time and space. Since the celebrating community is a society, all the patterns and structures of human social behavior come into play when Christians assemble for ritual practices. Hence, we can say that a liturgical act, as a ritual practice, is an embodied action in which a "social occasion"[56] takes place. Liturgical celebration is, in fact, an extension of the community's culture expressed in ritual practices. This means the celebrating community expresses itself through its own gestures, acts, or cultural behavior, as ritual languages.

55. Heschel, *The Insecurity of Freedom*, 72; Heschel's italics.

56. Kavanagh, using Erving Goffman's description of social relationship, suggests that liturgical act (I would compare it with ritual act), as "social occasion," presents parallel to what Goffman describes as types of social relationships. As "social occasion," they are: (1) occasional—suggests that liturgy is *festive*; (2) formal—means that liturgy has a certain *order*; (3) repetitive and rhythmic—means that liturgy is *unifying*; and (4) about survival—suggests that has an *eschatological dimension*. See Kavanagh, *On Liturgical Theology*, 137–42.

As mentioned earlier, van Gennep examined rites of passage from many different cultural contexts and discovered that most rites of passage move through three distinct phases: "separation;" "transition;" and "incorporation." It was van Gennep who introduced the *transitional* phase observed in a *rite of passage* as marked by "liminality" or *limen* (meaning "threshold" in Latin). For him, change is marked by three phases: preliminal, liminal, and postliminal. He contends that, "the door [threshold] is the boundary between the foreign and domestic worlds in the case of an ordinary dwelling, between the profane and sacred worlds in the case of a temple. Therefore to cross the threshold is to unite oneself with a new world."[57] Victor Turner summarizes the three phases introduced by van Gennep: "The first phase (of separation) comprises symbolic behavior signifying the detachment of the individual or group either from an earlier fixed point in the social structure, from a set of cultural conditions (a "state"), or from both. During the intervening "liminal period, the characteristics of the ritual subject (the "passenger") are ambiguous; he passes through a cultural realm that has few or none of the attributes of the past or coming state. In the third phase (reaggregation or reincorporation), the passage is consummated."[58] A liminal phase is inevitably a transformative place. It happens through ritual practices in the ambit of cultural contexts.

Following van Gennep, Turner develops further the idea of liminality in his analysis of the changes in traditional societies. Turner analyzed the liminal period of in-betweenness as a transitional condition of being out of the usual structure in people's lives, a creative condition in which the experience of *communitas* can occur. Turner uses Martin Buber's definition of *community*[59] as reference for his own description of *communitas*. The main idea here is the social relationship "*with* one another of a multitude of persons."[60] Among the variety of concepts Turner applies to *communitas*, the one most relevant here is his affirmation that "communitas has an existential quality; it involves the whole man in his relation to other whole men."[61]

From my perspective, van Gennep's contribution brings to the conversation a cultural framework from which the community of faith can

57. Gennep, *Rites of Passage*, 20.
58. Turner, *The Forest of Symbols*, 94.
59. Buber's definition was already quoted in chapter 3.
60. Turner, *The Forest of Symbols*, 127.
61. Ibid.

assimilate the cultural/contextual-language level of ritual communication. From this level of ritual communication, the community affirms its own cultural identity as the foundation on which the two other levels of ritual communication (theology and ethics) happen. There are no theological and ethical (socio-political-economic) commitments apart from cultural realities. Thus, the community (1) recognizes and affirms its own cultural values (*separation*—preliminal phase); (2) interacts with other cultural values (*transition*—liminal phase); and (3) contextualizes in mutuality its renewed cultural identity (*incorporation*—postliminal phase).

Van Gennep is not alone in this task of studying the role of ritual in society. Along with him stand Mircea Eliade,[62] Victor Turner,[63] Mary Douglas,[64] Clifford Geertz,[65] as representative scholars who have documented the ritual life of people in cultural contexts. From their contributions, we have been exposed to the role of ritual in cultural identity, social structure, religious beliefs, and in the communal sense of belonging. The analysis of a societal group's ritual life also reveals its understanding of the origin of the cosmos, its mythological narratives, its sacred symbolisms, its hierarchical structures, and the significance of birth, life, and death as relevant moments of passage, transition, or transformation.

CONTRIBUTION OF MARCEL MAUSS

The third contribution to this discussion comes from Marcel Mauss, who presents an original ethnographic study of the institution of gift in different primitive and archaic cultures.[66] The relevance of this study for the argument of this book is related to its original critical investigation of the economic importance of gift and its role in ancient societies, which I believe has ethical implications for modern societies. Mauss' basic idea is that the exchange of gift, which he refers to as a *system of total services*, is part of a cyclically structured communication system of reciprocity sustained by the rule that

---

62. For reference on ritual, myth, symbol, religious history, and phenomenology of religion, see Eliade, *Images and Symbols*; Eliade, *Man and the Sacred*; Eliade, *The Sacred and the Profane*; Eliade and Apostolos-Cappadona, *Symbolism, the Sacred, and the Arts*; and Eliade and Trask, *Rites and Symbols of Initiation*.

63. Turner, *The Forest of Symbols*.

64. Douglas, *Cultural Bias*; and Douglas, *Natural Symbols*.

65. Geertz, *The Interpretation of Cultures*.

66. Mauss, *The Gift*.

each gift has to be reciprocated.[67] The system generates an obligation, an exchange. In his ethnographic study, Mauss argues that in ancient societies "exchanges and contracts take place in the form of presents; in theory these are voluntary, in reality they are given and reciprocated obligatorily."[68] Accordingly, these phenomena of exchange and contract in archaic societies present a different system of exchange from ours. They are *total* because "it is not individuals but collectivities that impose obligations of exchange and contract upon each other."[69] He argues that all social phenomena are connected with each other in totality. The gift is only one part of this total social phenomenon. In archaic societies, a gift must be reciprocated or paid back; otherwise the *system of total services* is broken. In order to keep communal prestige, one must give; otherwise one loses reputation. The same can also be said for the obligation to receive. One has no right to refuse a gift. Refusing a gift would mean that one is afraid of having to reciprocate. When someone accepts a gift, this means that he or she also accepts the obligation to reciprocate.

Mary Douglas, who wrote the forward for the 1990 English edition of *The Gift*, begins by saying, "Charity is meant to be a free gift, a voluntary, unrequited surrender of resources."[70] She also says, "The theory of the gift is a theory of human solidarity."[71] For her, charitable foundations, some of which are "required to give away large sums as the condition of tax exemption,"[72] should not confuse donations with gifts. In her understanding of Mauss' approach to the matter, there should not be such a thing as a free gift. In her view, "What is wrong with the so-called free gift is the donor's intention to be exempt from return gifts coming from the recipient. Refusing requital puts the act of giving outside any mutual ties . . . A gift

---

67. This is a very complex concept that has in itself ethical implications for social, economic, political, legal, and religious issues. Mauss proposes to call this system "potlatch," which "essentially means 'to feed,' 'to consume.'" These *total services* and *counterservices*, says Mauss, "are committed to in a somewhat voluntary form by presents and gifts, although in the final analysis they are strictly compulsory, on pain of private or public warfare . . . The most important feature among these spiritual mechanisms is clearly one that obliges a person to reciprocate the present that has been received." See Mauss, *The Gift*, 5, 7.

68. Ibid., 3.

69. Ibid., 5.

70. Ibid., vii.

71. Ibid., x.

72. Ibid., vii.

that does nothing to enhance solidarity is a contradiction."[73] Again, these questions arise: What is a gift? Can we think of a gift outside the idea of "value"? What are the theological implications inherent in the concept of gift? Even though it is clear that theology is not Mauss' central focus (his argument is rather a positivist ethnographic discussion about politics and economics) it is possible to bring it into dialogue with the theological perspective of "symbolic exchange." Douglas says, "The theory of the gift is a theory of human solidarity."[74]

The schema that Mauss uses to illustrate what I am describing as socio/ political/economic language level of ritual communication is represented in his tripartite system of obligations: the obligation to *give*, to *receive*, and to *reciprocate*. My theological assumption is that God, as creator and sustainer of the universe, is the One who gives, and we are the receivers. In such a position, therefore, we have an obligation to return. Moreover, a community of faith must embrace and articulate these concepts subsequently incorporating them as part of its own practice. Acts of giving and offering ought to be understood in the context of symbolic exchange. For instance, one can ask: Is the liturgical act of offering understood and practiced in its fullness as gift or as donation? Does it have the characteristics of tax exemptions or the characteristics of symbolic exchange? These questions have ethical implications. In my view, Mauss suggests an ethical approach to human relationship that can be extended to the level of Christian prophetic engagement in society. Ritual practices can communicate ethical meanings, but they need to be explained through mystagogy—catechesis. In this regard, L. Edward Phillips writes:

> Despite the insistence of some liturgical theologians and ritologists that liturgy 'forms' ethical behavior, without proper catechesis liturgy will not be sufficient as an agent of ethical formation, as the overwhelming testimony of church history bears witness. Wealthy Christians all too easily can participate in the Eucharist with poor Christians and not understand the justice issues inherent in this act. Christians can pray, 'give us this day our daily bread,' and not understand the limits this places on the consumption of food resources . . . Therefore, today, as in the fourth century, the ethical relevance of liturgy must be periodically explained in order for worshipping Christians to make the connection.[75]

73. Ibid.
74. Ibid., x.
75. Phillips, "Liturgy and Ethics," 97.

Ritual praxis can communicate and form ethical behavior, but, as Phillips maintains, rituals are not sufficient as agents of ethical formation. The community of faith needs to engage in a pedagogical process of learning in order to examine and to discern the fullness of Christian life that bears witness to a transformed ethical attitude. A community that engages in acts of love and justice, solidarity and peace, and equality and fraternity, having the prophetic reference of acting justly, loving tenderly, and walking humbly before God and human beings, demonstrates concretely that it has assimilated the concept of gift in its totality.

In reflecting on the contributions of Mauss, which in its turn reflects on the contributions of J. Baudrillard's, Chauvet suggests, "The *gift* is without doubt what, among our institutions, best resists the imperialism of 'value.' . . . It has neither utility value nor commercial value, but only 'the value of symbolic exchange.' . . . Because it is some object which 'one lets go as if it were a part of oneself,' it becomes a signifier that 'grounds both the presence of one to the other and their absence from one another.'"[76] Because this process functions outside the order of value, it opens the possibility to theologically conceive of this symbolic exchange between God and humankind through *grace*. Chauvet also affirms: "Therefore, theologically, grace requires not only this initial gratuitousness on which everything else depends but also the graciousness of the whole circuit, and especially of the return-gift. This graciousness qualifies the return-gift as beyond-price, without calculation—in short, as a response of love. Even the return-gift of our human response thus belongs to the theologically Christian concept of 'grace.'"[77]

Using Mauss' ideas as model, Chauvet comes to the conclusion that there is no materialistic reception of anything as a gift, which does not require some return-gift as a sign of gratitude, at the very least a 'thank you' or some facial expression. This underscores the idea that the gesture of exchanging gifts carries the obligation of the return-gift as a response.

As we saw in chapter two, at Jesus' Table the community performs a communal remembrance of Jesus' offering for others. Because Christ's body is given to us, we are challenged to give our lives as return-gifts for the nourishment of others. What we see in creation is God's hospitability,

---

76. Chauvet is indebted not only to Mauss's *The Gift*. He also makes use of Baudrillard's *Pour une critique de l'économie politique de signe*. For a discussion on the contributions of both authors in Chauvet's work, see Chauvet, *Symbol and Sacrament*, 103.

77. Ibid., 108–9.

where no juridical, economic, or political powers subvert God's unconditional gift. In creation, as at Jesus' Table, there are no value exchanges to perpetuate dominion. God's hospitable symbolic exchange expressed in creation, and Jesus' self-offering at the table, are the theological references for a prophetic practice of symbolic exchange.

At the beginning of his book, Mauss presents two foundational questions that guide his study: "What rule of legality and self-interest, in societies of a backward or archaic type, compels the gift that has been received to be obligatorily reciprocated? What power resides in the object given that causes its recipient to pay it back?"[78] His conclusion is, "Societies have progressed in so far as they themselves, their subgroups, and lastly, the individuals in them, have succeeded in stabilizing relationships, giving, receiving, and finally, giving in return."[79] So, one asks: How can the idea of symbolic exchange work when we consider market interest as the principle for relations between individuals, groups, and nations? A possible answer, following Mauss' reasoning, is already before us, i.e., "in peace that has been imposed, in well-organized work, alternately in common and separately, in wealth amassed and then redistributed, in the mutual respect and reciprocating generosity that is taught by education."[80] This is why, for me, Mauss' study has ethical implications, an ethic of symbolic exchange, that seeks to remind all of us of our symbolic standing in relation to others.

From the perspective of living a faithful and prophetic Christian life in the world, we are challenged to celebrate the sacraments through commitment to a liturgical spirituality, that is, a prophetic praxis directed to the well-being of humankind. This is our call, a call toward unity, reconciliation, and transformation. This assumption is rooted in Scripture (God's gift, which brings unity); Sacraments (Christ's paschal mystery, which brings reconciliation); and Ethics (Spirit's breath, which brings transformation).

The juxtaposition of these three concepts provides a theoretical framework for my idea of *total sacramental rituality*. My approach to this theoretical paradigm is that, in celebrating the sacraments, a community of faith experiences in totality a transformative reality in a given culture. God's gifts are "separated" (given), received (liminal transition), and reciprocated (incorporation in mission) in cyclical ritual actions that (1) affirm God's project of life for the whole creation; (2) support the spiritual life

78. Mauss, *The Gift*, 3.

79. Ibid., 82.

80. Ibid., 83.

of the celebrating community; (3) value the community's cultural context; and (4) challenge the community of faith to be an agent of social-political-economic transformation. From this perspective it is possible to say that the sacramental life of the church has the potential of transforming an old oppressive reality into a new redemptive experience of liberation. It is a transposition from an old state without God's presence (total gift) to a renewed state with God's mercy: God's self-giving. The prophetic community is called to act with ethical commitment against so many factors that compromise the dignity of human beings and the stability of the created order. It is by celebrating a living sacramental life that the community internalizes the most fundamental expression of transformation. The prophetic community is a transformative community—a visible sign of *total sacramental rituality*: theology, culture, and ethics. Next chapter will explore what I am calling *A Matrix of Total Sacramental Rituality*. We will travel together in spiritual prophetic journey as we reflect on the beauty of sacramental theology—the paradigm for prophetic liturgy seeking transforming Christian praxis.

5

A Matrix of Total Sacramental Rituality

Help us accept each other as Christ accepted us;
teach us as sister, brother, each person to embrace.
Be present, Lord, among us and bring us to believe
We are ourselves accepted and meant to love and live.

Teach us, O Lord, your lessons, as in our daily life
we struggle to be human and search for hope and faith.
Teach us to care for people, for all, not just for some,
to love them as we find them or as they may become.

Let your acceptance change us, so that we may be moved
in living situations to do the truth in love;
to practice your acceptance, until we know by heart
the table of forgiveness and laughter's healing art.

Lord, for today's encounters with all who are in need,
who hunger for acceptance, for righteousness and bread,
we need new eyes for seeing, new hands for holding on;
renew us with your Spirit; Lord, free us, make us one!

Fred Kaan[1]

THIS IS A HYMN of gathering, caring, acceptance, and commitment. Is not that what prophetic liturgy is all about? Is not that what we experience in sacrament? Is not that a representation of what happens in ritual practice? A close reading of this poem reveals parallels to these concepts. Its content

---

1. United Methodist Church (U.S.), *The United Methodist Hymnal*, 560.

discloses the in-depth meaning of Christian life. It challenges our Christian praxis, as a prophetic community of faith, as a society that seriously wants to be part of and to promote God's project for humanity: abundant life. In sum, Kaan's poem is a prophetic prayer for the unity and mission of Christ's Body. Thus, it connects us to the concept of *total sacramental rituality*. Why did I choose a poem, a song, to introduce the *matrix of total sacramental rituality*? The simplest reason is because poems are born in human desire. They are variations on a given theme. The *matrix of total sacramental rituality* is born in spiritual prophetic desire. It is a variation and repetition of a given theme: the beauty of sacramental theology. Rubem Alves speaks to this approach to beauty, variation, and repetition when he says:

> Beauty always demands repetition. Beauty is infinite; it is never satisfied with a final form. Every experience of beauty is the beginning of a new universe. This is why the same theme must be repeated, every time in a different form. Every repetition is the resurrection of a past experience which must remain alive. The same poem, the same music, the same story . . . And yet, they are never the same, every time fresh, every time new . . . Every repetition is a disappointment; it has the flat taste of 'déjà vu.' The excitement of the first time is gone forever. But beauty is different. Every time it is repeated, the body reverberates again. The ecstasies of love always longs for its return.[2]

The *matrix of total sacramental rituality* is a complex schema of different tripartite forms. The tripartite schema of *beauty, variation,* and *repetition* is one of them.

The interconnection of these concepts provides the active and dynamic understanding, in totality, of the sacramental life of the church: prophetic Trinitarian spirituality. In the preceding chapter, we saw that the references for a prophetic Christian practice are theology, culture, and ethics. These are the foundations on which to build the *matrix*. That is, they provide a skeleton that sustains the concept of *total sacramental rituality*. The *matrix* has the concept of sacrament as its nest where the theological, cultural, and ethical understandings are nurtured. They all reach their maturity in sacramental practice. I will return to this concept later. For now, I provide a brief theological analysis of the content of Kaan's text. In principle, this should help toward understanding the matrix.

---

2. Alves, *The Poet, the Warrior, the Prophet,* 124–25.

THEOLOGICAL REFLECTION ON KAAN'S POEM

The first stanza of Kaan's poem says that we need help. When the reference for our practice in the world is Christ himself, we need help. To accept another person "as Christ accepted us" is not an easy task to face. Jesus embraced all kinds of people. He gathered with children, women, men, political and religious authorities, strangers, prostitutes, the sick, the poor, and the miserable.[3] When we embrace people without prejudice, we are manifesting our belief in Christ's *total* ministry—Christ's ultimate desire that we all may be sisters and brothers, embracing each other in mutual relationship of love, peace, and justice. Our relationship with our neighbor is one of many ways to testify how we understand and follow Christ's *total* teachings. Kaan suggests that the presence of Jesus Christ in our midst will help us to *believe, love* and *live,* another foundational tripartite schema of the matrix.

The second stanza emphasizes the experience of Jesus' teachings in all circumstances of our daily life. Jesus' teachings challenge our human nature. That is why Kaan talks about the "struggle to be human." The connection between the "struggle to be human" and the "search for hope and faith" is strong evidence of Kaan's social and religious consciousness. In this sense, he explores the spirituality incarnated in human relationships through unconditional love: "to care for people, for all, not just for some . . . as we find them or as they may become." The tripartite schema in this stanza can be delineated as *faith, hope,* and *care.*

The third stanza emphasizes transformation. There is a perception that we need to be changed "to do the truth in love." That change depends on acceptance, and it is a continuous action in living situations. In practicing Christ's acceptance, "until we know by heart," we continuously reveal our changing. It must happen in the here and now of our time: in our family, in our communities, in our society, in the world. Kaan affirms that this changing is not just a rational, a cognitive matter, but mainly, it touches human sensitivity: "until we know by heart." Thus, we will change ourselves and we

---

3. Dom Hélder Câmara makes a distinction between poverty and misery. He says, "I shall care for the poor, being particularly concerned that poverty should not degenerate into misery. Poverty can and at times must be accepted generously or offered spontaneously as a gift to the Father. But misery is degrading and repellent; it destroys the image of God that is in each of us; it violates the right and duty of human beings to strive for personal fulfillment" (see Schipani and Wessels, *The Promise of Hope,* 123).

will be mediators of transformation in our world. The tripartite form I see in this stanza is *truth*, *forgiveness*, and *healing*.

The fourth stanza is the culmination of the prophetic sense of this hymn. It is a prayer directed to the Prophetic God, the transcendent righteousness, the only One who can give "new eyes for seeing, new hands for holding on." It is directed to the only One who can transform us by the work of the Holy Spirit. A renewed community is able to see "who are in need, who hunger for acceptance, for righteousness and bread." As a prophetic community, we must go out to see, to accept, and to hold. We remember the words of Jesus Christ reclaiming the prophet Isaiah saying, "The Spirit of the Lord is upon me, because he has anointed me to bring good news to the poor. He has sent me to proclaim release to the captives and recovery of sight to the blind, to let the oppressed go free, to proclaim the year of the Lord's favor." (Luke 4:18–19) The last sentence in Kaan's poem, "Lord, free us, make us one!" impels us, as prophetic community, to be free from the evil of division, prejudice, intolerance, inequality, and exclusivity. Kaan's words are prophetic, a hymn of transformation that celebrates the *oikoumene* where, in Christ, there is a place for everyone. The tripartite schema in this stanza is *righteousness*, *bread*, and *freedom*.

All of these concepts, which I am designating as "tripartite schema," provide a configuration of important parts of the *matrix of total sacramental rituality*. In its essence, the *matrix of total sacramental rituality* is a complex of religious concepts. The following graphic shows the Trinitarian dimension of the *matrix*. As in the concept of *perichoresis*, this *matrix* has the sense of mutuality and its distinct parts are not to be conceived separately without their interchangeable connections. As a complex of concepts, the matrix is not closed; equal relevant elements could be added.

THE MATRIX OF TOTAL SACRAMENTAL RITUALITY

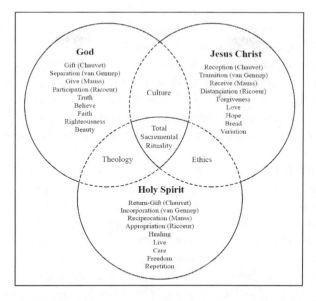

This *matrix*, which I have constructed from a variety of theological, socio-logical, anthropological, poetical and hermeneutical concepts, presented by a selected group of thinkers, is a variation of what I characterized as *the structure of prophetic vocation* in Chapter Three. *Total sacramental rituality* happens in the context of prophetic vocation. Much of what characterizes this *matrix* was touched on in previous chapters. Nonetheless, it is impor-tant to emphasize that the *matrix* incorporates in itself the idea of total-ity. This is primarily revealed in the *perichoretic* concept of the Trinity. As I mentioned before, the trinitarian element I am suggesting is based on Chauvet's system of symbolic exchange. My assumption is that a prophetic community of faith practices *total sacramental rituality* when it recognizes and accepts: (1) that the Scripture is a living Word of God for us today, which needs to be prophetically proclaimed; (2) that liturgical and sacra-mental celebrations reclaim the memory of the life, death, and resurrection of the Son of God, which needs to be remembered constantly; and (3) that a Christian human ethic, personal and communal, must be a response to the work of the Holy Spirit, which needs to be revealed in serving each other without prejudice.

The Trinitarian approach I am suggesting, which is not explicitly described and developed in Chauvet's symbolic exchange system, can be structured as follows: God—Scripture—The author and giver of the Word; Jesus Christ—Sacraments—The reference and receiver of sacramental life; Holy Spirit—Ethics—The intercessor and mediator of return-gift in ethical praxis. This assumption is rooted in Scripture—God's gift, which brings the sense of belonging; Sacraments—Christ's paschal mystery, which brings reconciliation; and Ethics—Spirit's breath, which brings transformation. In order to be authentically *whole*, the *matrix of total sacramental rituality* needs to incorporate the *perichoretic* inclusivity of the Triune God. Three liturgical actions may enhance our understanding of the principle suggested here: adoration, praise, and invocation. First, we *adore* the Triune God for what God is. God is the creator, the sustainer, the *tremendous*, and so on. God is the source of our worship in the sense of adoration. The act of adoration implies glorification, honor and reverence for God. It also includes merit, value, consideration, importance, dignity, excellence and appreciation. When we adore God, we recognize the attributes of God. God is holy, almighty, powerful, great, creator, etc. For all that God is, we adore God, we worship God. Therefore, in adoration, we express recognition of God's sovereignty, greatness, and holiness. It is our recognition of God as *Tremendum*, the *Lumen*, and the *Wholly Other*, to use the words of the phenomenology of religion.[4] In recognition and respect, we stay in awe before God—the *tremendum*. That is why we sing: "Holy, holy, holy, God of power and might." The beauty of God's creation, the revelation of God's presence in the history of humanity, and God's commandment for love, justice, and peace invite us to adore the God of power and might, to bow down with respect, and to be amazed and inspired by God's presence. Because of what God is, we adore God.

Second, we *praise* the Triune God because we celebrate the self-giving God, incarnated and revealed in our lives. The act of praise implies in jubilation, joy, and gratitude. Praise is the supreme expression of gratitude to God for God's unconditional love for all creation. We praise God for everything that God does in our environment, for all that God has given us—the fruit of God's everlasting goodness and grace, through the life and ministry of Jesus Christ. In return, we offer our lives and gifts as an expression of our gratitude for God's grace, favor, and blessings. That is why we have the freedom to sing with joy and shouts, in thanksgiving for what God has done in the community, in the world, in God's creation. We celebrate

4. See Otto, *The Idea of the Holy*, 12–24.

the God that walks with us, close to our side, who knows our struggle, our cries, and our claims—a friendly God as on the road to Emmaus.

Third, we *invoke* the Triune God because we need winds of life to strengthen us as we worship God and offer ourselves to be used for God's mission. Anointed and blessed by the power of the Holy Spirit, we move forward as witnesses of transformation in the world. And for that we say, "come, Holy Spirit, come!" This is the *epiclesis* not only over the Eucharistic elements or over the water. The *epiclesis* happens whenever we are gathered together as community of faith, whenever we are sent out in God's mission, whenever we visit the sick, and pray for healing. The Holy Spirit goes with us whenever we march for justice and peace, whenever we vote, whenever we stand up for the cause of the afflicted, the oppressed, and the disenfranchised. When we invoke the Holy Spirit, we must be prepared to be transformed and to be agents of transformation.

An important guiding principle to conceive the concept of the *matrix of total sacramental rituality* is that we are a community of people, and, as such, we need to recognize the *whole* of human existence not as separate culture, separate ethnicity, separate gender, separate language, and separate social-political-economic class. When we acknowledge the whole of human existence, we are enabled to see that every human being has the same need for food, shelter, clothing, health, education, etc. In sum, a human being is born naked, breathes the same air, and dies as anyone else does. We are different and yet equals under God's grace.

Another important principle present in the *matrix* is that through prophetic liturgical praxis, God's people affirms its intercultural identity, renews its spiritual life (sacramental understanding), commits to the well being of the whole creation, proclaims its interconnectedness as Church—the Body of Christ (baptismal covenant), mediates transformation through prophetic actions, and celebrates the enjoyment of being God's children regardless of race, gender, age, sexual orientation, or social-political-economic-educational background.

As mentioned before, the *matrix* was constructed on the basis of the influence of a variety of theological, sociological, and anthropological concepts seeking inquiry into the prophetic dimension of the liturgy. I am convinced that prophetic liturgy contributes to the establishment of political-social-economic justice, equal opportunities, inclusive actions, and any other actions that affirm the human being's dignity and the dignity of the whole creation. As community of faith, aware of the prophetic dimension of its liturgy, the community wrestles against the oppression of political-so-cial-economic unjust systems, and focuses its prophetic praxis as mediation of transformation of such systems. It is time now to return to some of the questions presented at the beginning of this book: How can a liturgy be pro-phetic? What does liturgy have to do with political-social-economic justice and action? How does prophetic liturgy engage the community as agent of transformation? Does the way Christian communities celebrate challenge them to be agents of transformation? What are the biblical, historical, and theological references for a prophetic liturgy? These questions, among oth-ers, are not rhetorical questions. They emphasize the relevance of spiritual consciousness—a spirituality that is rooted in prophetic sensitivity. This perspective explores the interrelationship of liturgy and theology as they interact with the human and social science fields. The complexity of the *matrix* is centered on the conception that liturgical praxis and theological understanding should construct spiritually engaged consciousness in the whole community of faith, committed to the well being of all people and the created order, prophetically claiming political-social-economic justice. Christian liturgical praxis, as ritual acts, are places for constructing an ef-fective human consciousness in terms of being an active participant in the spiritual and the concrete world. The variety of liturgical language present in the liturgical praxis such as music, gesture, icons, words, to name some, facilitate (construct) our growing in the Christian life as well as in our way to live in the concrete world.

All of this expresses the meaning of the word "total" in the *matrix*. It is one thing to write about how liturgical praxis forms and transforms indi-viduals and communities toward responsible participation in social, politi-cal, and economic life. It is quite another thing to make it true and viable. Thus, we need to reflect about how liturgical praxis might be employed as a responsible and feasible means of formation and transformation. The key to transformation, renewal, and unity in the church community is a living liturgy where corporate liturgical praxis such as praying, singing, reading, greeting, embracing, contemplating, reciting, acting, dancing, serving, receiving, blessing, and going forth, encourage the community of faith to put into practice its own vocation of welcoming all together in response to Jesus' prayer "that they may be one." The result is a living celebration of life—a communal encounter with God, with oneself, and with others.

The main goal of the *matrix of total sacramental rituality* is to pro-vide the prophetic community of faith with alternative references for its

Christian sacramental identity through praxis both inside and outside the church. The alternatives presented in this book can be summarized as follows: (1) Ritual and people doing transformative work; (2) Personal engagement in prophetic praxis; (3) A prophetic community as God's gift for the life of the world; (4) Formation of agents of transformation; and (5) Liturgical praxis calling for the fulfillment of mission. What follows is a reflection on each of these alternatives, offering additional concepts involved in understanding the practical dimension of the *matrix*.

RITUAL AND PEOPLE DOING TRANSFORMATIVE WORK

It is only by active participation that one can fully understand ritual acts. In phenomenology of religion, ritual is conceived as the equivalent gesture of symbol. That is to say, ritual is the symbol acted. In this sense, as in the case of symbol, ritual is the primary language of religious experience. It reflects sacred relationships. Ritual works to nurture the sense of belonging. Through ritual acts the community of faith constructs an effective human consciousness in terms of being active participants in the spiritual and concrete world. Therefore, ritual is participatory and transformative. It touches human senses, especially when the liturgical action is performed in the context of honoring loved ones. There is communication; there is a sense of belonging; there is a sense of real presence; there is a sense of life eternal. Performance in ritual celebration is to be experienced by the whole community. In prophetic sacramental ritual, there are no spectators. We are all ritual performers. Embodied action demands integral participation, not only in the sense that everybody participates, but also in the sense that the whole individual body participates in it. In the context of a prophetic Christian community, ritual praxis engages the community in deep relationship with the Triune God and with others. There is communication; there is a sense of belonging. Ritual works to nurture identity. Through ritual acts, the community of faith constructs an effective human consciousness in terms of being active participants in the spiritual and concrete world. Ritual does its transformative work as people participate in it.

Rituals are fertile grounds for teaching and learning. In fact, teaching and learning are not disconnected from each other. Through rituals, the community of faith constructs knowledge together in mutual relationship, mutual commitment, and mutual desire to grow. There is a juxtaposition of mutual learning as we interact and construct knowledge in a safe place, where participation is genuinely invited. Currently, it is well accepted that there are different types of knowledge generated through social relationships. In the context of the church environment, we may say that ritual engagements, where social relationships are manifested, are constructive places to generate knowledge.

Christian liturgical practices, as ritual acts, are places for constructing an effective human consciousness in terms of being an active participant in the spiritual and concrete world. The variety of cultural languages present in liturgical praxis such as music, gesture, icons, and words, among others, can facilitate growth in our Christian life as well as how we live in the world. A prophetic liturgical celebration that manifests socio-cultural sensitivity and is grounded in consistent theological paradigms is destined to be an agent of transformation. Thus, the liturgical praxis—meaning all communication acts in the whole celebration—give meaning and identity to the community, challenging its participants to share what has been learned and experienced. It means that rituals are educational, pastoral, and theological activities. They reflect who we are (culture), where we are (*habitus*), how we are (habit), and point us towards what we are called to be. In short, our celebrations become places of catechesis in which we learn who and whose we are, as well as for what purpose we are, before God and humanity.

The beauty of ritual is that it connects us in a wide circle of celebration, joining all members of Christ's Body in one accord, made up of different notes, which resound as grandiose hums echoing love, peace, justice, and equality. The result is a living celebration of life—a praise to God. In my view, a prophetic liturgical celebration, a prophetic ritual, can be the dialogical ground where Church and world come together, embracing each other in songs of Christ's body, the ultimate reference for the social body.

PERSONAL ENGAGEMENT IN PROPHETIC PRAXIS

In his book *Render Unto God*, James Newton Poling challenges us to prophetic practice. He says:

> How do we begin to make changes in the way we think, live, and pray so that the love and power of God are more real in our lives? How do we understand the steps in our own transformation that move us toward an inclusive community of loving justice across barriers of gender? I believe that the transformation we seek is a gradual process of opening ourselves to the grace of God,

receiving the witness from those for whom God has made "a way out of no way," and accompanying those who have gained wisdom from their journey. Those who know God's love and power the best are seldom given high status by a world in which the values of competitive greed and violent domination rule. Those who know God best are often surprising: the vulnerable stranger who asks for a place to stay; the wise prisoner who has no hope of being released; the survivor of violence who knows the depths of evil and the resilience of the human spirit.[5]

From a practical theology standpoint, Poling is presenting a move from personal to communal transformation that shows a deep prophetic consciousness. A variation on Poling's thoughts could be that prophetic transformation starts in an open heart and mind whose eyes are directed toward God, whose ears are open to hear Jesus' message, whose human sensitivity is empowered by the work of the Holy Spirit, and whose passion for justice, love, peace, equality, solidarity, etc. is so contagious that she or he cannot control her or himself until other human beings join in the "dance." Prophetic self-consciousness is contagious and through it, transformation can reach geometrical proportions.

The first practical element of the *matrix*, then, is personal engagement in prophetic praxis. This assumption calls us to participate actively in the life of the faith community and in the life of the community outside. It implies developing critical consciousness with the ability to see reality, to judge its effects, and to act for the well being of human dignity and the created order. Prophets are often regarded as "counter-voices," "counter-culture," which speak for the weak, the oppressed, and the marginalized mediating God's desire for the well-being, for the life, and for the beauty of the whole creation. There is risk in making option for prophetic praxis because it goes beyond the comfortable zone of spiritual and political alienation. It can be both a rich and a tragic experience at once—rich when there is respect and openness to differences, and tragic when sectarian and individualistic interests and practices speak louder than engagement in a genuine process of learning that is not rooted in personal or partial levels of interest.

5. Poling, *Render Unto God*, 235. In the sequence of this chapter (page 236), Poling develops what he calls the "nine-stage theory of spiritual growth," in which he describes "the process of transformation available to all persons who respond to the needs of others." The nine stages are: (1) Open Receptivity; (2) Listening and Believing; (3) Seeking Knowledge; (4) Courage to Act; (5) Accompaniment; (6) Transformation of Self and Congregation; (7) Making Long-term Commitments; (8) Prophetic Action; and (9) Transformation of Worship and Community Life.

One of the challenges church leaders face, from this prophetic meth-odological perspective, is to provide the community with social-economic justice awareness, historical-cultural interconnectedness, global-ecumeni-cal praxis, and yet, at the same time, allow the community to affirm its own tradition, spirituality, and religious values, as it interacts with differences while exploring inculturation in its ultimate level. In sum, we need the spirit of the prophets with the capacity to see reality from God's perspec-tive, the ability to analyze the social-political-economic contexts in light of God's perspective, and the courage to act towards dialogical transformation of such reality.

Prophetic liturgical praxis is fecund ground s for developing critical consciousness. That means, the church community needs to experience the liturgy that teaches, the liturgy that challenges, the liturgy that mediates social-political-economic dialogical engagements as a result of its spiritual commitments. We, liturgists and ministers, need access to the historical-critical method, with all its variation, in order to broaden our vision of the historical context in which we live. Historical criticism is especially relevant in the liturgical field given the fact that liturgical experiences are produced and performed in a specific historical-social context (*Sitz im leben*). This is possible through interaction in a diverse environment, interdisciplin-ary conversation, and inclusive dialogue. From the practical stand point, the community of faith will, then, deliberately involve each member in prophetic praxis with a sense of purpose beyond his or her own personal embedded world view. It is important to assure that liturgical celebrations contribute to the establishment of engaged spiritual consciousness of the whole community of faith—a community that is committed to the well-being of all people and the created order. Personal engagement in prophetic praxis, as described here, challenges our embedded spiritual-theological constructs, broadens our view of the world, and encourages all of us to actively participate in God's work in the world.

A PROPHETIC COMMUNITY AS GOD'S GIFT FOR THE LIFE OF THE WORLD

A prophetic community is committed to the sacramental understanding of itself as God's gift for the life of the world. This theological approach leads us to transformation. Consequently, it is possible to say that a prophetic community is a sign of the *Passover*. In this sense the prophetic community has the potential to transform an old oppressive reality into a new redemptive experience of liberation. Through its prophetic praxis, the church can become the bridge over which society finds its way to social justice, to peace, to environmental equilibrium, to fair political relations, and to sustainable economic development. As God's gift for the life of the world, the prophetic community is called to act with commitment against all signs of anti-life that compromise the dignity of humanity and the stability of the created order.

In general, words, gestures, body movements, symbols, songs, smells, tastes, and other kinds of ritual language expressions tend to address the community's faith and spiritual growth more than its rational and cognitive development. This is not to imply that the community does not need spiritual growth. To be able to transform and to be transformed, the community of faith needs both Pentecost and Armageddon. From Pentecost, it experiences the ultimate level of intimacy with God, and from Armageddon, the community learns the ultimate level of human suffering. Thus, what is at stake here is the *focus* and *locus*. The challenge is to make connections between both realities through better appropriation of language. One can learn from the other so that participants can be both spiritually blessed and conscientiously prepared to act in mission in the world.

My contention is that transformative liturgy transcends personal "cloistered" spirituality. Transformative communities are fecund grounds, which work to overcome "cloistered" spirituality and move the community towards legitimate outward patterns of transformation. This is a necessary distinction precisely because the dichotomy of supernatural/natural forms lines of division between liturgical praxis of what is "spiritual" and what is "secular;" the former related to atemporal realities—the transcendent, the supernatural, the sacred—and the latter related to temporal realities—the political sphere, the natural, the worldly, the secular, the autonomous, and the historical. Therefore, transforming liturgical praxis must take into account the juxtaposition of spiritual realities, which bring peace (a state of spirit), and natural realities, which bring justice (a state of life). Since the ultimate goal of the prophetic praxis is the announcement of a kin-dom of peace, which presupposes the establishment of justice, the juxtaposition of both realities is imperative in transforming liturgy, literally as God's gift for the life of the world.

Prophetic liturgical praxis can address those realities. According to Gutiérrez's liberation framework, what we need is a "vital attitude,

all-embracing and synthesizing, informing the totality as well as every de-
tail of our lives; we need a 'spirituality.'"[6] He continues, "A spirituality is a
concrete manner, inspired by the Spirit, of living the Gospel; it is a definite
way of living 'before the Lord,' in solidarity with all human beings, 'with
the Lord,' and before human beings."[7] My view is that this spirituality is a
result of a transformative liturgy. It happens in the encounter of the axes
of Christian life and temporal experience. It is a juxtaposition of devotion,
prayer, commitment, and prophetic action. Therefore, a prophetic liturgical
praxis must communicate dimensions of both the spiritual and the concrete world.

The community of faith needs to ask herself whether her liturgical
praxis changes her way to live, to see, to confront, and to affirm life in the
social construct in which she lives. In the prophetic sense, we are all called
to be an agent of transformation in this world. We are called to affirm God's
unconditional love for everyone, without prejudice or preconditioned pre-
conceptions. We are called to establish justice and peace in any corner we
can reach. In sum, to be God's gift for the life of the world, the community
of faith is expected to operate in such a way that her theology and liturgical
praxis helps to develop in each member a constructive and transformative
engagement as citizens of this world.

When the community of faith sees herself engaged in prophetic praxis,
she promotes the ideal level of becoming God's gift for the life of the world.
She becomes sacramental to the world—means of God's grace, blessings,
and favor—a place where subjective and invisible concepts find their meanings in concrete and visible transformative life experiences. As community
of faith we need to work towards this goal more and more. In fact, this is the
ultimate goal of the *matrix of total sacramental rituality*.

FORMATION OF AGENTS OF TRANSFORMATION

The preparation of agents of transformation, who stand as prophets in solidarity with all in need, involves radical revisions of the inherited patterns of
education for church leadership, both clergy and laity. On the basis of education for critical consciousness, the community will be able to explore new
alternatives and patterns for the building of a just, participatory and sustainable community committed to the well being of humanity in its totality.

6. Gutiérrez, *A Theology of Liberation*, 117.

7. Ibid., 118.

Thus, the community of faith needs to evaluate its process of learning, considering: theological background, culture, and socio-economic context. In that sense, the teaching process has to be related: (1) to its spiritual fount of formation, (2) to the affirmation of community identity, and (3) to its critical political-pedagogical function. A process of learning with a critical consciousness happens through active social interaction where the method of *see*, *judge*, and *act* is referential for transformation. This mystagogical catechesis comes after ritual experiences, not before. Since ritual praxis enable growth, the formation for transformation also grows through ritual experiences. For example, one of the most significant mediums for formation and transformation is found in hymns, songs, and canticles.

The majority of contemporary Christians, young or old, educated or not, would not be able to explain in depth the meaning of the church's theological treatise, but all of us, certainly, would be able to talk about living liturgical experiences like, for example, the meaning of the hymns' doctrinal contents. As Ruth Duck observes, "Hymns give voice to faith in cultural forms through the style of both music and words."[8] Hymns have the subtle power of communicating deep truths through their words, sounds, and images. In other words, hymns teach! In order to be even more effective in the process of learning—of Christian formation—the hymns, as liturgical language, need to address the fullness of the liturgical purpose. Hymns, as liturgical language, can communicate theology, affirm the community's cultural identity, and eternalize transcendent liturgical expressions. Likewise, the message embodied in the artistic form must also be taken seriously and responsibly. As Frank Burch Brown reminds us in *Inclusive Yet Discerning,* "nothing one can say in words can exhaust the meanings and enjoyments music conveys, or can explain fully the sense of things its artful sounds can bring into being . . . the intrinsic power and inexplicable 'meaning' of music should cause worshipers to listen even more carefully to music's inner voice so as to discern how each kind or work of music enters and forms hearts and minds."[9] Therefore, in the midst of a time in which the variety of liturgical languages available to us is unparalleled in human history, there are some questions that require responsible answers: Which voices? What theology? Whose culture? Which *ordo*? What taste? The community of faith ought to be attentive to the language applied in its liturgical

---

8. Duck, *Finding Words for Worship*, 103.
9. Brown, *Inclusive yet Discerning*, 44–45.

praxis, understanding that they are mediums through which faith may be communicated, not ends unto themselves.

Another important aspect of the formation character of the liturgical praxis is that each liturgical expression needs to be carefully chosen in order to be both inclusive and diverse. Prophetic liturgical praxis is necessarily multicultural, intercultural, and intergenerational in its character and intention. Because of its multicultural character, this element may be utilized in ways that are both sensitive and simple. Let me offer one personal example. For those of us who are living in a foreign land, to hear somebody asking us to pray the Lord's Prayer in the language of our heart has tremendous impact in terms of human and spiritual sensitivity. In such a case, the matter of inclusiveness becomes not just some sympathetic sensibility. When inclusiveness is experienced in its fullness, when one is asked to pray in her or his own language, the community absorbs in totality God's care and love for all God's children. This assumption can be applied to gender, aging, race, education, sexual orientation, and socio-economic principles. As I see it, the very theological foundation for inclusivity is the redemptive character of Christ's incarnation in a segregated world. Redemption, by definition, stresses the inner concept of reversion; reversion from the undesirable state of death to the liberation of life, and from the addiction of injustice to the pleasure of breaking the walls of human segregation. Viewed from this perspective, the question should not be, "How does the regular liturgy form and transform individuals and communities toward inclusive participation in the world?" Instead, the question should be asked passionately and vociferously, "How does it not?" Thus, the question is about references. We, as people of God, need better references. We need appropriate pedagogical approaches. We need solid "food," meaning effective liturgical celebrations, which foster both teaching and learning. Approached from this perspective, the faith community inevitably must touch on the issue of liturgical praxis as fertile ground for formation and transformation, another key element of the *matrix of total sacramental rituality.*

LITURGICAL PRAXIS CALLING FOR THE FULFILLMENT OF MISSION

Each and every liturgical celebration of the church should send all its participants out to work for the fulfillment of mission in the world. The regular Sunday service does not end with the postlude. The service needs to be seen as a well around which the community gathers in order to be nurtured and revitalized for prophetic action in and for the world. Our lives are a continuing act of worship. It is in this gathering around the sacred well that the prophetic community of faith finds grace to articulate its mission, harmonized with the gospel it preaches, and conformed to the Christ it proclaims. Prophetic mission is directly connected with the praxis of justice. Liturgy expresses and fosters faith that does justice in mission praxis. In my understanding, there is no prophetic mission that is isolated from efforts to restructure the social-political-economic order. The justice that Christians proclaim in mission is integrally connected to the idea that the struggle for a just social-political-economic order parallels the struggle for the dignity of the whole human being. The theological foundation for Christians' practice of justice is God's saving work through grace. God's acts of justice are full of love, mercy, and forgiveness. God's act of justice is a gift through which God redeems God's own creation. These truths need to be embodied in prophetic mission.

In being involved with the concept of the *matrix of total sacramental rituality* one is challenged to be ready to offer oneself to others. This has to do with our call to be a prophetic community of faith. This is a call to stay alert, vigilant, holding oneself in readiness to be an agent of transformation, an agent in God's mission. The community of faith transforms as it is transformed. It is a cyclical process that never ends precisely because creation is dynamic and active. Our readiness demands a radical and disciplined life.

Among other important liturgical praxis, preaching and praying are the two liturgical languages with special implications for the mission of the church. Peter Paris, describing the similarities between preaching and praying, makes an insightful comment about presenting a prophetic language for the proclamation of the Word and prayer. He says: "The aim of both [preaching and prayer] is to bring comfort to the sorrowful, uplift to the weary, encouragement to the disappointed, faith to the despairing, courage to the weak, repentance to self-destructive sinners who either ignore or betray God's way of life. In addition to this pastoral mission, both praying and preaching have a prophetic aim, namely, to condemn every form of racism, both in thought and in practice."[10] A prophetic celebrating community is committed to those on the margins, who are frequently the voiceless. In that sense, besides this pastoral mission suggested by Paris, a prophetic liturgy has a political connotation. At this juncture stands the

---

10. Paris, "The Linguistic Inculturation of the Gospel," 94.

issue of our active political-spiritual participation in the life of the world. It represents our work for justice, mercy, and love, and envisions political transformation for the sake of future generations. As was emphasized in Chapter 1, Amos' prophetic voice must ring out incessantly in our ears, when we hear him saying that God hates, despises the festivals, and also when he affirms that God takes no delight in the community's solemn assemblies. God doesn't want to hear the noise of our songs, and God will not listen to the melody of our instruments. What must remain are the actions that let "justice roll down like waters, and righteousness like an ever-flowing stream" (Amos 5:21–24). Micah's reference "to do justice, and to love kindness, and to walk humbly with your God" (Mic 6:8) essentially provides a summary of the same idea. The socio-political content of these biblical passages, along with many others with prophetic implications, demands a responsible hermeneutical approach. Biblical scholars such as Kevin J. Vanhoozer present a postmodern hermeneutical perspective as an alternative means of reading texts in community. In this regard, for example, he agrees with "privileging the 'horizon' or 'intention' of the text rather than the author, and in viewing the text as a well of *possible* meaning from which diverse readers draw different interpretations. In short, the text has a sense potential, but actual meaning is the result of an encounter with the reader."[11] The community is a reading community that has the ability to inform readers and to facilitate their interpretations. Greater attention should be paid to how reading takes place in community and how texts might function in relationship to reading communities. The proclamation of the Word, as liturgical language, both reveals and transforms. That is, it opens new horizons of understanding for oneself, for the community, or for the world and, as a result of this revealing process, it transforms the reader's, the community's, or the world's existence.

In conclusion, when we inquire into the prophetic dimension of the liturgy utilizing the assumptions presented in this book as a theoretical framework, we find ourselves in a radical *matrix* that needs to be approached with an open mind. In this process we join together, first, in an engaging learning process in which the liturgical fundamentals and theological concepts need to be strongly emphasized. The content needs necessarily to be structured in dynamic correlation with the common Christian tradition, to the here and now, and to the eschatological dimension of the liturgy—its spiritual relevance for future generations. In this sense, Saliers'

---

11. Vanhoozer, *Is There a Meaning in This Text?*, 106.

view of eschatological understanding is indispensable. He says: "In the eschatological art faithfully celebrated, in every time and place and culture, human ears hear things that speak what no ear has yet heard, human eyes see things that manifest that which no eye has yet seen. But such seeing and hearing is faithful when what is prayed becomes a way of justice and mercy. The foretaste of glory divine nurtures the fruits of the Spirit in human history. God's promises hold the future, calling us to taste and see, to work and pray."[12] As prophetic community of faith, we are responsible for the eschatological hope; we are agents of God's love, justice and beauty; we are prophets reclaiming life for all, not just for some.

Second, in order to answer questions such as "who are we before God," the community of faith needs to assess its direct connection with the "cultures" within the worshiping community. Mark Francis helps us articulate this assumption. He says: "The more 'culturally sensitive' in the parish often contend that for liturgy to be effective, it must incorporate customs and folk rites borrowed from the various cultures present in the parish."[13] The community of faith with culture sensitivity welcomes differences with open arms, without prejudice. It is not difficult to perceive the community, or even an individual, who values cross-cultural experience and expresses it through ritual actions. For example, the passing of Christ's peace, the prayers of the people, the use of foreign languages in songs and in Scripture readings, to name just a few liturgical actions, are signs of culture sensitivity and means of God's welcoming grace—safe place for transformation.

Finally, a prophetic liturgy involves acquaintance with the practical dimension of the celebrating community, i.e. the subjective spiritual world is not disconnected from the concrete living world. In other words, *total sacramental rituality* facilitates the community's awareness of the trajectory of Christian history, the consciousness of its cultural unity, and attentiveness to the transformative prophetic dimension of Christian liturgical praxis in the world. One simple sentence conveys the whole of this book: *Ubi caritas et amor Deus ibi est.*[14]

---

12. Saliers, *Worship as Theology*, 230.

13. Francis, *Liturgy in a Multicultural Community*, 9.

14. Possible English translation: Where charity and love abide, God dwells there.

Bibliography

Adam, A. K. M. *What Is Postmodern Biblical Criticism?* Minneapolis: Fortress, 1995.

Adams, Walter Randolph, and Frank A. Salamone. *Anthropology and Theology: Gods, Icons, and God-Talk*. Lanham, MD: University Press of America, 2000.

Alves, Rubem A. *I Believe in the Resurrection of the Body*. Philadelphia: Fortress, 1986.

———. *The Poet, the Warrior, the Prophet*. Philadelphia: Trinity, 1990.

———. *What Is Religion?* Maryknoll, NY: Orbis, 1984.

Anderson, E. Byron. *Worship and Christian Identity: Practicing Ourselves*. Collegeville, MN: Liturgical, 2003.

Anderson, E. Byron, and Bruce T. Morrill, eds. *Liturgy and the Moral Self: Humanity at Full Stretch before God: Essays in Honor of Don E. Saliers*. Collegeville, MN: Liturgical, 1998.

Anderson, Herbert, and Edward Foley. *Mighty Stories, Dangerous Rituals: Weaving Together the Human and the Divine*. San Francisco: Jossey-Bass, 1998.

Aune, David Edward. *Prophecy in Early Christianity and the Ancient Mediterranean World*. Grand Rapids: Eerdmans, 1983.

Baptism, Eucharist and Ministry. Geneva: World Council of Churches, 1982.

Batstone, David B. *Liberation Theologies, Postmodernity, and the Americas*. London: Routledge, 1997.

Benedict, Daniel T., Jr. *Come to the Waters: Baptism and Our Ministry of Welcoming Seekers and Making Disciples*. Nashville: Discipleship Resources, 1996.

Blount, Brian K., and Leonora T. Tisdale. *Making Room at the Table: An Invitation to Multicultural Worship*. Louisville: Westminster John Knox, 2001.

Boff, Clodovis. *Como Trabalhar Com Os Excluídos*. São Paulo: Paulinas, 1998.

Boff, Leonardo. *Ecclesiogenesis: The Base Communities Reinvent the Church*. Maryknoll, NY: Orbis, 1986.

———. *Holy Trinity, Perfect Community*. Maryknoll, NY: Orbis, 2000.

———. *Liberating Grace*. Maryknoll, NY: Orbis, 1979.

———. *Sacraments of Life, Life of the Sacraments*. Washington, DC: Pastoral, 1987.

———. *Trinity and Society, Theology and Liberation Series*. Maryknoll, NY: Orbis, 1988.

———. *Way of the Cross: Way of Justice*. Maryknoll, NY: Orbis, 1980.

Bonino, Míguez, José. *Faces of Latin American Protestantism: 1993 Carnahan Lectures*. Grand Rapids: Eerdmans, 1997.

———. *Rostros Del Protestantismo Latinoamericano*. Buenos Aires: Nueva Creación, 1995.

Bibliography

Borgen, Ole E. *John Wesley on the Sacraments: A Theology Study*. Reprint, Eugene: Wipf and Stock Publishers, 2000.

Bosch, David J. *Transforming Mission: Paradigm Shifts in Theology of Mission*. Maryknoll: NY: Orbis, 1991.

Bradshaw, Paul F., Bryan D. Spinks, and Ronald Claud Dudley Jasper. *Liturgy in Dialogue: Essays in Memory of Ronald Jasper*. London: SCPK, 1993.

Brinkman, M. E. *Sacraments of Freedom: Ecumenical Essays on Creation and Sacrament Justification and Freedom, Iimo Research Publications [Interuniversitaire Instituut Voor Missiologie En Oecumenica] [Formerly: Iimo Research Pamphlets]*. Zoetermeer, Netherlands: Meinema, 1999.

Brockman, James R., ed. *The Church Is All of You: Thoughts of Archbishop Oscar Romero*. Minneapolis: Winston, 1984.

Brown, Frank Burch. *Good Taste, Bad Taste, and Christian Taste: Aesthetics in Religious Life*. New York: Oxford University Press, 2000.

———. *Inclusive yet Discerning: Navigating Worship Artfully*. Grand Rapids: Eerdmans, 2009.

Browning, Robert L., and Roy A. Reed. *The Sacraments in Religious Education and Liturgy: An Ecumenical Model*. Birmingham, AL: Religious Education, 1985.

Buber, Martin. *Between Man and Man*. Trans. Ronald Gregor Smith. New York: Macmillan, 1972.

———. *The Prophetic Faith*. New York: Harper, 1960.

Burrow, Rufus. *God and Human Dignity: The Personalism, Theology, and Ethics of Martin Luther King, Jr.* Notre Dame, IN: University of Notre Dame Press, 2006.

———. *Martin Luther King, Jr. for Armchair Theologians*. Louisville: Westminster John Knox, 2009.

Buyst, Ione. *Los Símbolos En La Liturgia*. México: Dabar, 1998.

Câmara, Hélder, and Francis McDonagh. *Dom Helder Camara: Essential Writings*. Maryknoll, NY: Orbis, 2009.

Casel, Odo. "Mystery and Liturgy." In *Primary Sources of Liturgical Theology: A Reader*, ed. Dwight W. Vogel, 29–35. Collegeville, MN: Liturgical, 2000.

Cavanaugh, William T. *Torture and Eucharist: Theology, Politics, and the Body of Christ*. Malden, MA: Blackwell, 1998.

Chauvet, Louis-Marie. "Rituality and Theology." In *Primary Sources of Liturgical Theology: A Reader*, ed. Dwight W. Vogel, 193–99. Collegeville, MN: Liturgical, 2000.

———. *Symbol and Sacrament: A Sacramental Reinterpretation of Christian Existence*. Collegeville, MN: Liturgical, 1995.

Chupungco, Anscar J. *Cultural Adaptation of the Liturgy*. New York: Paulist, 1982.

———. *Liturgical Inculturation: Sacramentals, Religiosity, and Catechesis*. Collegeville, MN: Liturgical, 1992.

———. *Worship: Beyond Inculturation*. Washington, DC: Pastoral, 1994.

Collins, Mary. *Worship: Renewal to Practice*. Washington, DC: Pastoral, 1987.

Comblin, José. *Retrieving the Human: A Christian Anthropology*. Maryknoll, NY: Orbis, 1990.

Connerton, Paul. *How Societies Remember*. New York: Cambridge University Press, 1989.

Croatto, José Severino. *Los Lenguajes De La Experiencia Religiosa: Estudio De Fenomenologia De La Religión*. Buenos Aires: Docencia, 1994.

Crockett, William R. *Eucharist, Symbol of Transformation*. New York: Pueblo, 1989.

Crosby, Michael. *House of Disciples: Church, Economics, and Justice in Matthew.* Maryknoll, NY: Orbis, 1988.

Dalmais, Irénée Henri. "The Liturgy as Celebration." In *The Church at Prayer: An Introduction to the Liturgy,* ed. Aimé George Martimort and trans. Matthew J. O'Connell, 233–43. Collegeville, MN: Liturgical, 1987.

————. "The Liturgy as Celebration." In *Primary Sources of Liturgical Theology: A Reader,* ed. Dwight Vogel, 18–26. Collegeville, MN: Liturgical, 2000.

Daly, Herman E., John B. Cobb, and Clifford W. Cobb. *For the Common Good: Redirecting the Economy toward Community, the Environment, and a Sustainable Future.* Boston: Beacon, 1989.

Derrida, Jacques. *The Gift of Death.* Chicago: Universty of Chicago Press, 1995.

Douglas, Mary. *Cultural Bias.* London: Royal Anthropological Institute, 1978.

————. *Natural Symbols: Explorations in Cosmology.* New York: Pantheon, 1970.

Driver, Tom F. *Liberating Rites: Understanding the Transformative Power of Ritual.* Boulder, CO: Westview, 1998.

Duck, Ruth C. "Expansive Language in the Baptized Community." In *Primary Sources of Liturgical Theology: A Reader,* ed. Dwight W. Vogel, 286–94. Collegeville, MN: Liturgical, 2000.

————. *Finding Words for Worship: A Guide for Leaders.* Louisville: Westminster John Knox, 1995.

————. *Gender and the Name of God: The Trinitarian Baptismal Formula.* New York: Pilgrim, 1991.

Duck, Ruth C., and Patricia Wilson-Kastner. *Praising God: The Trinity in Christian Worship.* Louisville: Westminster John Knox, 1999.

Dussel, Enrique D. *Ethics and Community, Theology and Liberation Series.* Maryknoll, NY: Orbis, 1988.

Echols, James. *I Have a Dream: Martin Luther King Jr. and the Future of Multicultural America.* Minneapolis: Fortress, 2004.

Eliade, Mircea. *Images and Symbols: Studies in Religious Symbolism.* New York: Sheed & Ward, 1961.

————. *Man and the Sacred: A Thematic Source Book of the History of Religions.* New York: Harper & Row, 1974.

————. *The Sacred and the Profane: The Nature of Religion.* New York: Harper, 1961.

Eliade, Mircea, and Charles J. Adams. *The Encyclopedia of Religion.* Vol. 12. New York: Macmillan, 1987.

Eliade, Mircea, and Diane Apostolos-Cappadona. *Symbolism, the Sacred, and the Arts.* New York: Crossroad, 1985.

Eliade, Mircea, and Willard R. Trask. *Rites and Symbols of Initiation: The Mysteries of Birth and Rebirth.* New York: Harper & Row, 1965.

Empereur, James L., and Christopher Kiesling. *The Liturgy That Does Justice.* Collegeville, MN: Liturgical, 1990.

Francis, Mark R. *Liturgy in a Multicultural Community.* Collegeville: Liturgical, 1991.

Freire, Paulo. *Education for Critical Consciousness.* New York: Seabury, 1973.

————. *Pedagogy of the Oppressed.* Trans. Mary Bergman Ramos. New rev. 20th anniversary ed. New York: Continuum, 1997.

Fretheim, Terence E. *God and World in the Old Testament: A Relational Theology of Creation.* Nashville: Abingdon, 2005.

Bibliography

Gadotti, Moacir. *Pedagogy of Praxis: A Dialectical Philosophy of Education, Suny Series, Teacher Empowerment and School Reform*. Albany: State University of New York Press, 1996.

Geertz, Clifford. *The Interpretation of Cultures*. New York: Basic, 2000.

Gennep, Arnold van. *Rites of Passage*. Chicago: University of Chicago Press, 1984.

Goll, Jim W., and Michal Ann Goll. *Compassion: A Call to Take Action*. Shippensburg, PA: Destiny Image, 2006.

Guardini, Romano. "The Playfulness of the Liturgy." In *Primary Sources of Liturgical Theology: A Reader*, ed. Dwight W. Vogel, 38–45. Collegeville, MN: Liturgical, 2000.

Gutiérrez, Gustavo. "Renewing the option for the Poor." In *Liberation Theologies, Postmodernity, and the Americas*, ed. David B. Batstone, 69–82. London: Routledge, 1997.

———. *A Theology of Liberation: History, Politics, and Salvation*. Maryknoll, NY: Orbis, 1988.

———. *We Drink from Our Own Wells: The Spiritual Journey of a People*. Maryknoll, NY: Orbis, 1984.

Hahn, Carl Joseph. *História Do Culto Protestante No Brasil*. São Paulo, Brasil: ASTE, 1989.

Hanson, Geddes W. "'Multicultural' Worship: A Careful Consideration." In *Making Room at the Table: An Invitation to Multicultural Worship*, ed. Brian K. Blount and Leonora T. Tisdale, 145–61. Louisville: Westminster John Knox, 2001.

Hauerwas, Stanley, and Samuel Wells. *The Blackwell Companion to Christian Ethics*. Malden, MA: Blackwell, 2004.

Hellwig, Monika. *The Eucharist and the Hunger of the World*. Kansas City: Sheed & Ward, 1992.

Herzog, William R. *Jesus, Justice, and the Reign of God: A Ministry of Liberation*. Louisville: Westminster John Knox, 2000.

———. *Parables as Subversive Speech: Jesus as Pedagogue of the Oppressed*. Louisville: Westminster John Knox, 1994.

Heschel, Abraham Joshua. *The Insecurity of Freedom: Essays on Human Existence*. New York: Farrar, Straus & Giroux, 1966.

———. *The Prophets*. Vol. 2. New York: Harper & Row, 1962.

———. *The Prophets: An Introduction*. Vol. 1. New York: Harper & Row, 1962.

Heschel, Abraham Joshua, and Susannah Heschel. *Abraham Joshua Heschel: Essential Writings*. Maryknoll, NY: Orbis, 2011.

Irvin, Dale T. *Hearing Many Voices: Dialogue and Diversity in the Ecumenical Movement*. Lanham, MD: University Press of America, 1994.

Isasi-Diaz, Ada Maria. "Solidarity: Love of Neighbor in the 1980s." In *Lift Every Voice: Constructing Christian Theologies from the Underside*, ed. Susan Brooks Thistlewaite and Mary Potter Engel, 31–40. San Francisco: Harper & Row, 1990.

Johnson, Maxwell E. *The Rites of Christian Initiation: Their Evolution and Interpretation*. Collegeville, MN: Liturgical, 1999.

Johnson, Maxwell E., ed. *Living Water, Sealing Spirit: Readings on Christian Initiation*. Collegeville, MN: Liturgical, 1995.

Jones, L. Gregory, and Stephen E. Fowl, eds. *Rethinking Metaphysics, Directions in Modern Theology*. Oxford: Blackwell, 1995.

Kapferer, Bruce. *A Celebration of Demons*. Washington, DC: Smithsonian Institution Press, 1994.

Kavanagh, Aidan. *On Liturgical Theology, The Hale Memorial Lectures of Seabury-Western Theological Seminary,* 1981. New York: Pueblo, 1984.

————. *The Shape of Baptism: The Rite of Christian Initiation.* Collegeville, MN: Liturgical, 1991.

Kaylor, R. D. *Jesus the Prophet: His Vision of the Kingdom on Earth.* Louisville: Westminster John Knox, 1994.

King, Martin Luther, Jr. *The Trumpet of Conscience.* New York: Harper & Row, 1968.

LaCugna, Catherine Mowry. *God for Us: The Trinity and Christian Life.* San Francisco: HarperSanFrancisco, 1992.

Lathrop, Gordon. *Holy Things: A Liturgical Theology.* Minneapolis: Fortress, 1993.

Léonard, Émile-G. *O Protestantismo Brasileiro: Estudo de Eclesiologia e História Social.* São Paulo, Brasil: ASTE, 1963.

Long, D. Stephen. *Divine Economy: Theology and the Market.* Radical Orthodoxy. New York: Routledge, 2000.

Maldonado, Luis. *El Sentido Litúrgico: Nuevos Paradigmas.* Madrid: PPC, 1999.

Malina, Bruce J. *The Social Gospel of Jesus: The Kingdom of God in Mediterranean Perspective.* Minneapolis: Fortress, 2001.

Martimort, Aimé George *The Church at Prayer: An Introduction to the Liturgy.* Trans. Matthew J. O'Connell. Collegeville, MN: Liturgical, 1987.

Mauss, Marcel. *The Gift: The Form and Reason for Exchange in Archaic Societies.* London: Routledge, 2000.

McKenna, Megan. *Prophets: Words of Fire.* Maryknoll, NY: Orbis, 2001.

Mendonça, Antônio Gouvêa. *O Celeste Porvir: A Inserção Do Protestantismo No Brasil.* São Paulo, Brasil: Paulinas, 1984.

————. *Protestantes, Pentecostais e Ecumênicos: O Campo Religioso e Seus Personagens.* São Bernardo do Campo: UMESP, 1997.

Mendonça, Antônio Gouvêa, and Prócoro Velasques Filho. *Introdução Ao Protestantismo No Brasil.* São Paulo: Loyola, 1990.

Míguez Bonino, José. *Faces of Latin American Protestantism:* 1993 *Carnahan Lectures.* Grand Rapids: Eerdmans, 1997.

Milbank, John. "Can a Gift be Given? Prolegomena to a Future Trinitarian Metaphysics." In *Rethinking Metaphysics, Directions in Modern Theology,* ed. L. Gregory Jones and Stephen E. Fowl, 119–61. Oxford: Blackwell, 1995.

————. "Postmodern Critical Augustinianism." In *The Postmodern God: A Theological Reader, Blackwell Readings in Modern Theology,* ed. Graham Ward, 265–78. Malden, MA: Blackwell, 1997.

————. *The Word Made Strange: Theology, Language, Culture.* Challenges in Contemporary Theology. Cambridge: Blackwell, 1997.

Moltmann, Jürgen. *On Human Dignity: Political Theology and Ethics.* Philadelphia: Fortress, 1984.

————. *The Trinity and the Kingdom: The Doctrine of God.* San Francisco: Harper & Row, 1981.

————. "The Triune God: Rich in Relationships." *Living Pulpit* 8, no. 2 (1999) 4–5.

Moltmann-Wendel, Elisabeth, and Jürgen Moltmann. *Humanity in God.* New York: Pilgrim, 1983.

Monteiro, Simei Ferreira de Barros. "Singing a New Song: Developing Methodist Worship in Latin America." In *The Sunday Service of the Methodists: Twentieth-Century*

Worship in Worldwide Methodism: Studies in Honor of James F. White, ed. Karen B. Westerfield Tucker, 265–82. Nashville: Abingdon, 1996.

Norris, Kathleen. *The Cloister Walk*. New York: Riverhead, 1996.

Otto, Rudolf. *The Idea of the Holy: An Inquiry into the Non-Rational Factor in the Idea of the Divine and Its Relation to the Rational*. New York: Oxford University Press, 1950.

Outler, Albert Cook, and Richard P. Heitzenrater, eds. *John Wesley's Sermons: An Anthology*. Nashville: Abingdon, 1993.

Owensby, Walter L. *Economics for Prophets: A Primer on Concepts, Realities, and Values in Our Economic System*. Grand Rapids: Eerdmans, 1988.

Pannenberg, Wolfhart. *Anthropology in Theological Perspective*. Philadelphia: Westminster, 1985.

Paris, Peter J. "The Linguistic Inculturation of the Gospel." In *Making Room at the Table: An Invitation to Multicultural Worship*, ed. Brian K. Blount and Leonora T. Tisdale, 78–95. Louisville: Westminster John Knox, 2001.

Phillips, L. Edward. "Liturgy and Ethics." In *Liturgy in Dialogue: Essays in Memory of Ronald Jasper*, ed. Paul F Bradshaw and Bryan D. Spinks, 86–99. London: SPCK, 1993.

Pickstock, Catherine. *After Writing: On the Liturgical Consummation of Philosophy, Challenges in Contemporary Theology*. Challenges in Contemporary Theology. Malden, MA: Blackwell, 1998.

Poling, James N. *Render Unto God: Economic Vulnerability, Family Violence, and Pastoral Theology*. St. Louis: Chalice, 2002.

Power, David Noel. *The Eucharistic Mystery: Revitalizing the Tradition*. New York: Crossroad, 1992.

———. *Sacrament: The Language of God's Giving*. New York: Crossroad, 1999.

Rabaté, Jean-Michel, and Michel Wetzel, eds. *L'éthique du Don: Jacques Derrida et la Pensé du Don*. Paris: Métailié-Transition, 1992.

Ramshaw, Gail. *God Beyond Gender: Feminist Christian God-Language*. Minneapolis: Fortress, 1995.

Reily, Duncan Alexander. *História Documental Do Protestantismo No Brasil*. São Paulo, Brasil: ASTE, 1984.

———. "O Culto Protestante No Protestantismo Puritano-Pietista." *Estudos de Religião* 1, no. 2 (1985) 89–102, .

Ricoeur, Paul. *The Conflict of Interpretations: Essays in Hermeneutics*. Evanston< IL: Northwestern University Press, 1974.

———. *Interpretation Theory: Discourse and the Surplus of Meaning*. Fort Worth: Texas Christian University Press, 1976.

———. *The Rule of Metaphor: Multi-Disciplinary Studies of the Creation of Meaning in Language*. Toronto: University of Toronto Press, 1977.

———. *Time and Narrative*. Chicago: University of Chicago Press, 1984.

Saliers, Don E. "Liturgy and Ethics: Some New Beginnings." In *Liturgy and the Moral Self: Humanity at Full Stretch before God: Essays in Honor of Don E. Saliers*, ed. E. Byron Anderson and Bruce T. Morrill, 15–35. Collegeville, MN: Liturgical, 1998.

———. *Worship and Spirituality*. Akron, Ohio: OSL, 1997.

———. *Worship as Theology: Foretaste of Glory Divine*. Nashville: Abingdon, 1994.

Santa Ana, Julio de. *Good News to the Poor: The Challenge of the Poor in the History of the Church*. Maryknoll, NY: Orbis, 1979.

————. "Priest and Prophet." In *The Promise of Hope: A Tribute to Dom Hélder*, ed. Daniel S. Schipani and Anton Wessels, 9–21. Elkhart, IN: Institute of Mennonite Studies, 2002.

Santa Ana, Julio de, ed. *Sustainability and Globalization*. Geneva: WCC, 1998.

Schillebeeckx, Edward. *Christ the Sacrament of the Encounter with God*. New York: Sheed & Ward, 1963.

Schipani, Daniel S., and Anton Wessels. *The Promise of Hope: A Tribute to Dom Hélder*. Elkhart, IN: Institute of Mennonite Studies, 2002.

Schmemann, Alexander. *The Eucharist: Sacrament of the Kingdom*. Crestwood, NY: St. Vladimir's Seminary Press, 1988.

————. *For the Life of the World: Sacraments and Orthodoxy*. Crestwood, NY: St. Vladimir's Seminary Press, 1998.

————. *Introduction to Liturgical Theology*. Portland, ME: American Orthodox, 1966.

————. *The World as Sacrament*. London: Darton Longman & Todd, 1966.

Schnelle, Udo. *The Human Condition: Anthropology in the Teachings of Jesus, Paul, and John*. Minneapolis: Fortress, 1996.

Sobrino, Jon. *Archbishop Romero: Memories and Reflections*. Maryknoll, NY: Orbis, 1990.

————. *No Salvation Outside the Poor: Prophetic-Utopian Essays*. Maryknoll, NY: Orbis, 2008.

Searle, Mark. "Liturgy as Metaphor." *Worship* 55 (1981) 98–120.

Stookey, Laurence Hull. *Baptism: Christ's Act in the Church*. Nashville: Abingdon, 1982.

————. "Three New Initiation Rites." In *Living Water, Sealing Spirit: Readings on Christian Initiation*, ed. Maxwell E. Johnson, 274–91. Collegeville, MN: Liturgical, 1995

Tanner, Kathryn. *Theories of Culture: A New Agenda for Theology, Guides to Theological Inquiry*. Minneapolis: Fortress, 1997.

Teresa. *Love: The Words and Inspiration of Mother Teresa*. Boulder, CO: Blue Mountain, 2007.

Teresa, and José Luis González-Balado. *In My Own Words*. Liguori, MO: Liguori, 1996.

Thistlewaite, Susan Brooks, and Mary Potter Engel, eds. *Lift Every Voice: Constructing Christian Theologies from the Underside*. San Francisco: Harper & Row, 1990.

Tugwell, Simon. *Early Dominicans: Selected Writings*. New York: Paulist, 1982.

————. *Ways of Imperfection: An Exploration of Christian Spirituality*. London: Darton Longman and Todd, 1984.

Turner, Victor Witter. *The Forest of Symbols: Aspects of Ndembu Ritual*. Ithaca, NY: Cornell University Press, 1967.

Tutu, Desmond, and Douglas Carlton Abrams. *God Has a Dream: A Vision of Hope for Our Time*. New York: Doubleday, 2004.

United Methodist Church (U.S.). *The United Methodist Hymnal: Book of United Methodist Worship*. Nashville: United Methodist Pub. House, 1989.

Vanhoozer, Kevin J. *Is There a Meaning in This Text?: The Bible, the Reader, and the Morality of Literary Knowledge*. Grand Rapids: Zondervan, 1998.

Manuel A. Vásquez, *The Brazilian Popular Church and the Crisis of Modernity*. Cambridge: Cambridge University Press, 1998

Vattimo, Gianni. *The End of Modernity: Nihilism and Hermeneutics in Postmodern Culture*. Baltimore: Johns Hopkins University Press, 1991.

Verner, David C. *The Household of God: The Social World of the Pastoral Epistles*. Chico, CA: Scholars, 1983.

Vogel, Dwight W. *Food for Pilgrims: A Journey with Saint Luke*. Akron, Ohio: OSL, 1996.

Bibliography

Vogel, Dwight W., ed. *Primary Sources of Liturgical Theology: A Reader*. Collegeville, MN: Liturgical, 2000.

Vogel, Dwight W., and Linda J. Vogel. *Sacramental Living: Falling Stars & Coloring Outside the Lines*. Nashville: Upper Room, 1999.

Vogel, Linda Jane. *Rituals for Resurrection: Celebrating Life and Death*. Nashville: Upper Room, 1996.

Vogel, Linda Jane, and Dwight Vogel. *Syncopated Grace: Times and Seasons with God*. Nashville: Upper Room, 2002.

Waetjen, Herman C. *A Reordering of Power: A Sociopolitical Reading of Mark's Gospel*. Minneapolis: Fortress, 1989.

Ward, Graham, ed. *The Postmodern God: A Theological Reader*, Blackwell Readings in Modern Theology. Malden, MA: Blackwell, 1997.

West, Cornel. *Prophesy Deliverance!: An Afro-American Revolutionary Christianity*. 1st ed. Philadelphia: Westminster, 1982.

White, James F. *Introduction to Christian Worship*. Nashville: Abingdon, 1980.

———. *Sacraments as God's Self Giving: Sacramental Practice and Faith*. Nashville: Abingdon, 1983.

———. *The Sacraments in Protestant Practice and Faith*. Nashville: Abingdon, 1999.

Zimmerman, Joyce Ann. *Liturgy and Hermeneutics*. Collegeville, MN: Liturgical, 1999.

Index

Index